icons from
TE PAPA
Pacific

icons from
TE PAPA

Pacific

First published in New Zealand in 2006 by Te Papa Press
P O Box 467, Wellington, New Zealand

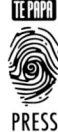

TE PAPA® is the trademark of the Museum of New Zealand
Te Papa Tongarewa

Te Papa Press is an imprint of the Museum of New Zealand
Te Papa Tongarewa

**National Library of New Zealand
Catalogue-in-Publication data**

Museum of New Zealand.
Icons from Te Papa : Pacific.
ISBN-13: 978-1-877385-25-4
ISBN-10: 1-877385-25-5
1. Museum of New Zealand – Catalogs.
2. Pacific Islanders – Material culture – Catalogs.
3. Islands of the Pacific – Antiquities – Catalogs. I. Title.
990.07493 – dc 22

Design by Mission Hall Creative
Photography by Michael Hall, Norman Heke, Jan Nauta
Digital imaging by Jeremy Glyde
Printed by Everbest Printing Co, China

Cover image:
Cloak
c. 1870
Rarotonga, Cook Islands
Cashmere wool, hibiscus fibre
1390 x 2180 mm
Gift of Te Aia Mataiapo, 1872

The Museum
of New Zealand
Te Papa Tongarewa

The Museum of New Zealand Te Papa Tongarewa offers visitors an encounter with Aotearoa New Zealand: its peoples and their histories, its cultures and art, and its natural environment.

The museum has had various identities over time. Established as the Colonial Museum in 1865, it was renamed the Dominion Museum in 1903 and the National Museum in 1972. Te Papa opened in 1998, combining the museum and National Art Gallery with a bold new conceptual approach.

Preserving and presenting the many strands of the nation's story is an essential expression of Te Papa's bicultural principle. This is based on a partnership between tangata whenua (Māori, the indigenous people) and tangata tiriti, the people living in this country by right of the Treaty of Waitangi, the founding document of the nation. Te Papa's collections reflect the diversity of this story.

This book draws attention to the Pacific, one of Te Papa's five major areas of scholarship, presenting highlights from that collection. These may be some of the museum's most treasured items, they may tell a tale of outstanding interest in itself, or they may capture the essence of a larger historical or cultural narrative.

If you have visited Te Papa, this book offers a record and a broader view of its treasures. If you are yet to visit, we hope it gives a flavour of the richness of life in this isolated group of Pacific islands.

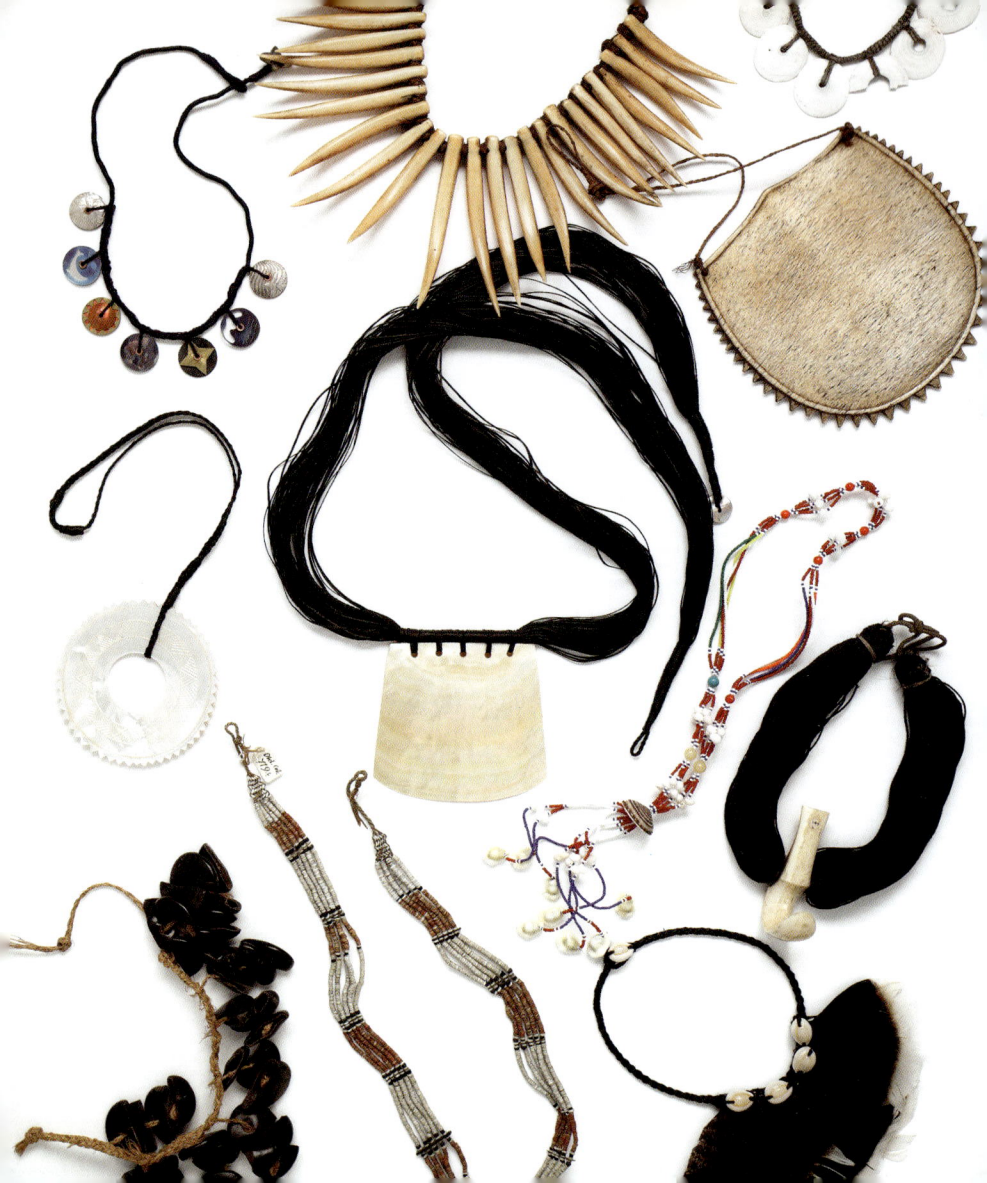

Te Papa's Pacific Collection

The Pacific collection consists of about 13 000 items from the many island groups of this vast ocean – ranging from the Federated States of Micronesia and Papua New Guinea in the west to Rapanui (Easter Island) in the east, and from Hawai'i in the north-east to New Caledonia in the south-west. Material from Indonesia, the Philippines, and Australia is not included, except for the Torres Strait Islands, which, though part of Australia, are culturally more aligned to Papua New Guinea.

For most of the museum's history, Pacific items have been part of what was known as the foreign ethnology collection. A small group of pieces from the Pacific (such as gifts to British administrators) came into the Colonial Museum in the nineteenth century, but more active collection development began with Augustus Hamilton, director of the museum from 1903. Hamilton deposited his own extensive collection of ethnographic material and encouraged others to donate theirs.

Body adornments from the Pacific.

In the twentieth century, the Pacific collection grew largely through donations. Among the most significant were gifts of Māori, Pacific, and North American items associated with James Cook's voyages of exploration. In 1912, Lord St Oswald, an Englishman, unexpectedly presented his family collection to the Dominion of New Zealand. Then, in 1955, the Imperial Institute in London (now the Royal Commonwealth Institute) gave an important group of items linked to the explorer James Cook; this had been in the possession of Queen Victoria and was presented to the institute by Edward VII. Cook himself may have given the items to George III after his second voyage. Two smaller gifts in 1947 and 1962 consist of items traceable to Cook's wife. Another major acquisition was the 1948 purchase by the New Zealand government of the Māori and Pacific collection of the London dealer W. O. Oldman. The Dominion Museum received most of the Māori, Marquesan, Admiralty Island, and New Caledonian pieces from this collection.

In 1991, as part of the development of Te Papa, a separate Pacific collection was established. It reflected a new approach to the representation of Pacific peoples in the national museum. Pacific peoples have now become well established in New Zealand; they are no longer foreigners, guest workers, or exotic peoples on remote islands, but neighbours, colleagues, and fellow citizens. Their objects and artworks are no longer simply comparative cultural specimens; they are the possessions and creations of known people.

The collection still documents a diverse island-based cultural heritage. But collection development has increasingly aimed to represent the visual culture and history of Pacific peoples in New Zealand. The scope ranges from new forms of weaving, tīvaevae (quilting), and tapa (bark cloth) to high fashion and contemporary art. Complicating this changed focus is the fact that many island-based communities have become more international in nature, as a result of air travel and new forms of communication. For example, a mat or quilt made by Tongan women in Los Angeles may be sent to Tonga as a gift and later brought to New Zealand to celebrate an important family event.

The selection of items in this book reflects the riches of this new diversity in the collection. Items made in the twenty-first century, with clearly identified histories, are included with pieces hundreds of years old, about which sometimes little is known. The selection also illustrates the diverse cultural histories of Pacific peoples over many centuries and records the fascination that their arts and customs had for those European observers and collectors who first came across them.

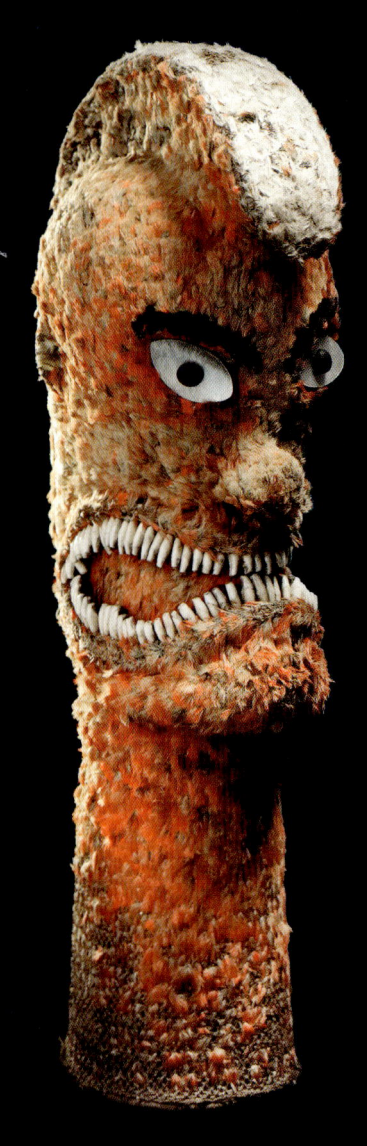

ʻaumakua hulu manu
(feathered god image)

Feathered god images from Hawaiʻi are believed to represent the war god Kūkāʻilimoko. Certainly, these bright and ferocious-looking figures are fitting for such a deity.

The images were made in a similar way to another noted form of Hawaiian artistry, the feathered helmet – a basketry frame was covered with fine netting, to which the feathers were attached. The eyes were cut pieces of pearl shell, set in place with wooden pegs representing the pupils. The mouth was furnished with a large number of dog teeth. Most feathered god images have a crest on the top and back of the head, similar to the crest on many Hawaiian helmets. Some have human hair attached in place of a feathered crest.

This image may have been collected on James Cook's third voyage (1776–79), but there is no specific evidence for this. Other ships called at the Hawaiian Islands in the late 1700s.

ʻaumakua hulu manu
(feathered god image)
late 18th century
Hawaiʻi
Split vine, plant fibre, feathers, shell, dog teeth
560 x 230 mm
Gift of Lord St Oswald, 1912

7

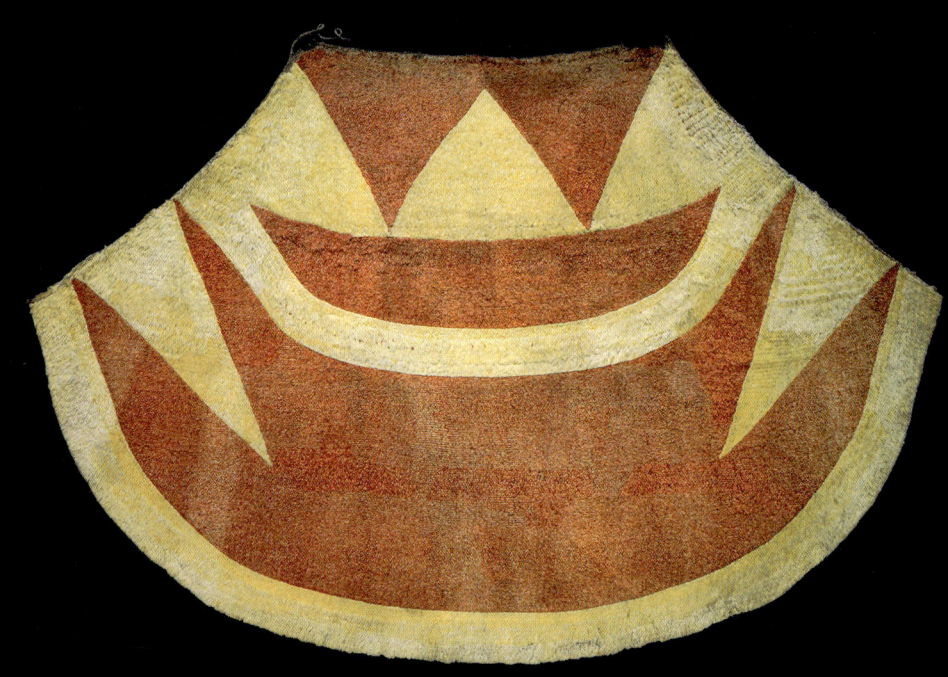

'ahu 'ula (feathered cloak)

On 26 January 1779, the Hawaiian high chief Kalaniʻōpuʻu took this cloak, which he was wearing, and draped it over the shoulders of Captain James Cook. He placed a feathered helmet on Cook's head, and laid several other cloaks at his feet. His people brought various offerings of food.

Less than three weeks later, Cook was killed at Kealakekua Bay, Hawaiʻi. The cloak and helmet were taken to England, and acquired by Sir Ashton Lever for his private museum. There, a picture of the cloak was painted by Sarah Stone, providing a record for confirming its subsequent movements.

The cloak and helmet were sold along with the other contents of the Leverian Museum in 1806, and later given to William Bullock, owner of another private museum. When his museum was sold in 1819, they were in a group of items purchased by Charles Winn, through whose grandson they came to New Zealand.

'ahu 'ula (feathered cloak)
late 18th century
Hawaiʻi
Plant fibre, feathers
1540 mm length, 2450 mm at widest part
Gift of Lord St Oswald, 1912

9

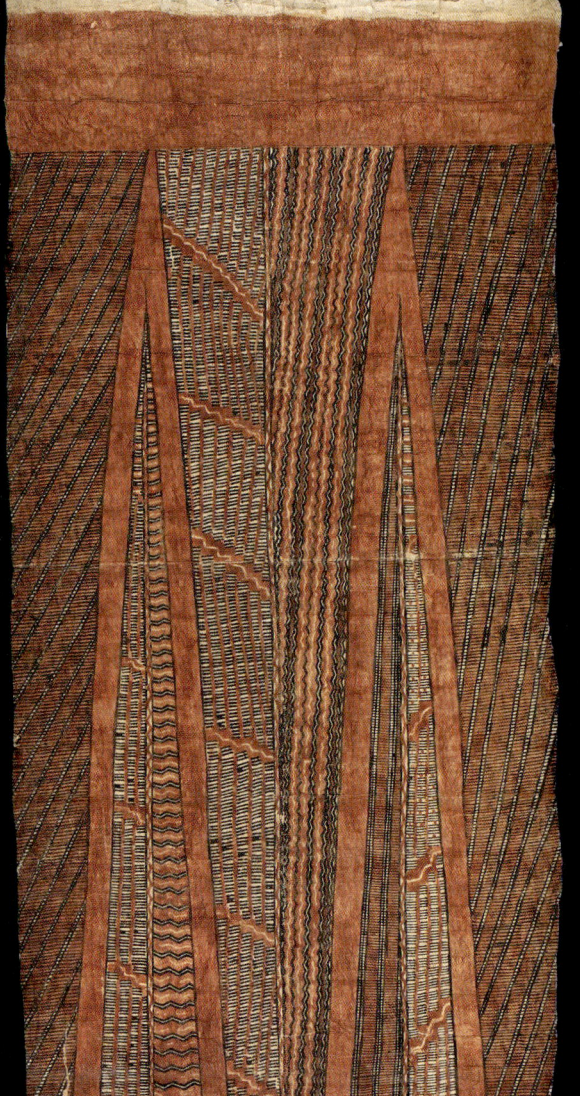

Kapa (bark cloth)

'It far surpasses any we have seen in the variety & beauty of its patterns, which often show an Elegance, & taste that would lead one to suppose their figures borrowed from the productions of more enlightened Nations: & seeing their strips exposd to sail [sic] at a distance, one might suppose oneself transported in a Linen drapers shop.'

So wrote Lieutenant Philip King during James Cook's 1776–79 voyage, describing Hawaiian kapa. 'They have a very great variety of patterns and many of them are extremely beautifull,' wrote the more prosaic Cook.

This is one of four pieces presented to the museum by the trustees of Alexander Turnbull's estate. It was noted at the time that they were collected during Cook's voyages. This has not been proven, although three of the pieces, including this one, have patterns typical of kapa known to have been collected by members of Cook's third expedition.

Kapa (bark cloth)
late 18th century
Hawai'i
Bark cloth
1290 x 635 mm
Gift of the Trustees of the Estate
of A. H. Turnbull, 1918

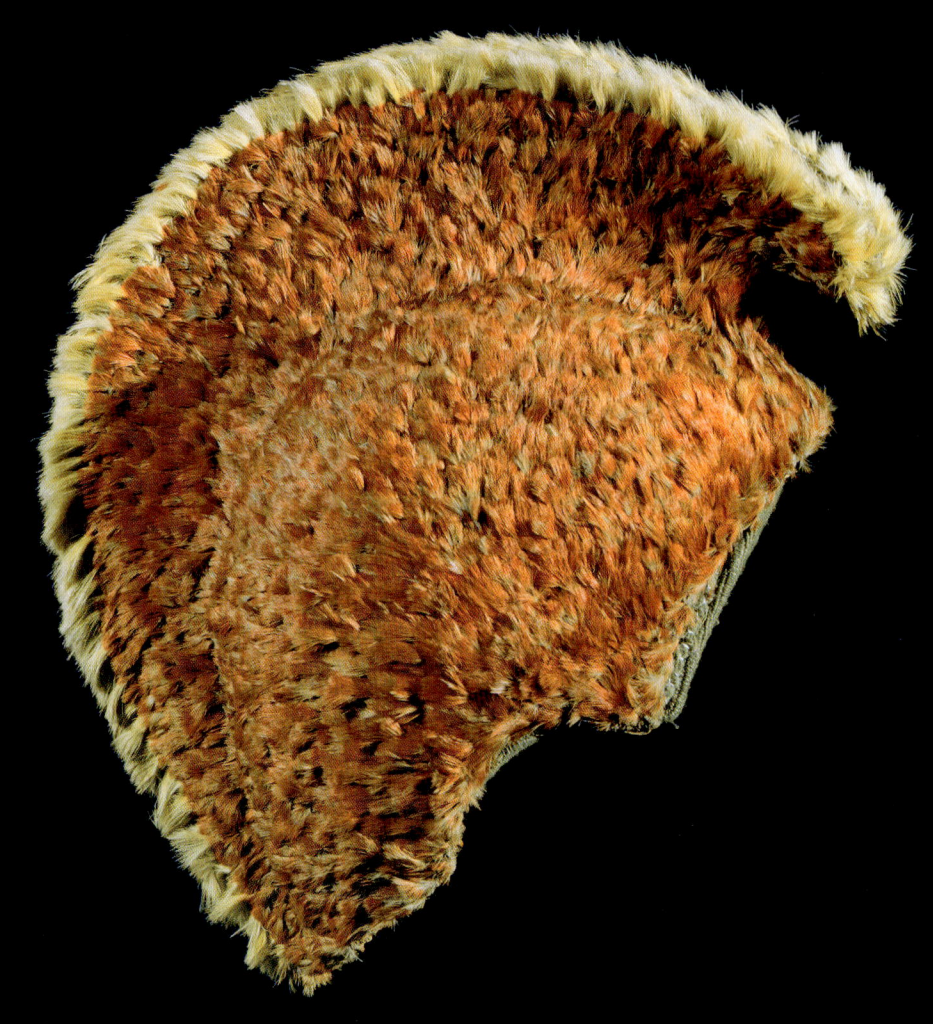

Mahiole (feathered helmet)

This helmet is believed to be the one placed on Captain James Cook's head by the Hawaiian high chief Kalaniʻōpuʻu on 26 January 1779. Like the cloak given to Cook at the same time, it is a product of extraordinary artistry. Its framework is covered with fine netting to which bundles of red feathers are attached. Yellow feathers decorate the central crest.

In the catalogue of the sale of Bullock's Museum in 1819, the helmet and cloak were described as follows: '34 The Feather Cloak, and Helmet ... are articles that must excite a melancholy interest in every spectator. They are the identical superb feather cloak which with the helmet, No. 1, were presented to the celebrated but unfortunate Captain Cook ... by the king of Owhyhee, who taking them from his own person ... placed them on the person of our great circumnavigator, as the highest mark of distinction he could bestow.'

Mahiole (feathered helmet)
late 18th century
Hawaiʻi
Split vine, plant fibre, feathers
Gift of Lord St Oswald, 1912

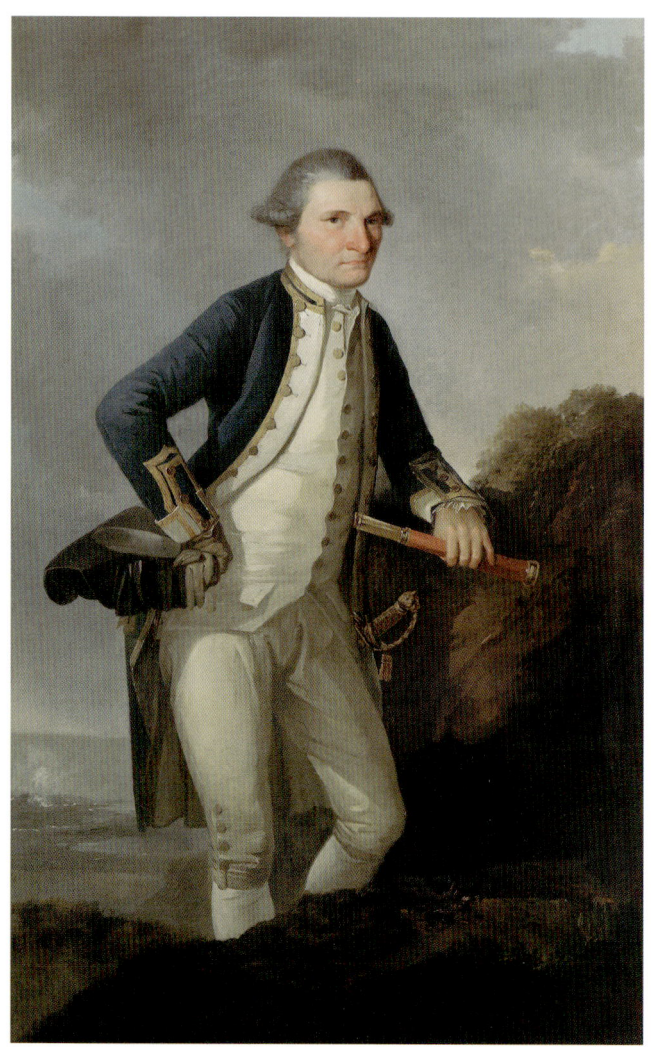

Captain James Cook

The British Admiralty and the Royal Society sent three voyages of discovery to the Pacific between 1768 and 1780, under the command of James Cook. The aims were geographic exploration and scientific observation, particularly in astronomy but also in natural history.

The artist John Webber sailed on the third Cook voyage. Cook's instructions required him to 'observe the Genius, Temper, Disposition, and Number of the Natives and Inhabitants, where you find any'. Webber's visual records of Pacific people and their environments are sympathetic, but they also conceal violence, hostage-taking, and the impacts of trade.

Webber portrays here the 'great circumnavigator' with the emblems of his role and authority: a naval uniform, sword, and telescope. His expression is stern, and his gaze piercing. This is the portrait of a hero, a representative of the European Enlightenment. It also depicts a commander who ordered Webber to suppress or ignore violent encounters.

John Webber
(1751–93), Switzerland/England
Portrait of Captain James Cook
1776
Oil paint on canvas
1094 x 692 mm
Gift of the New Zealand government, 1960

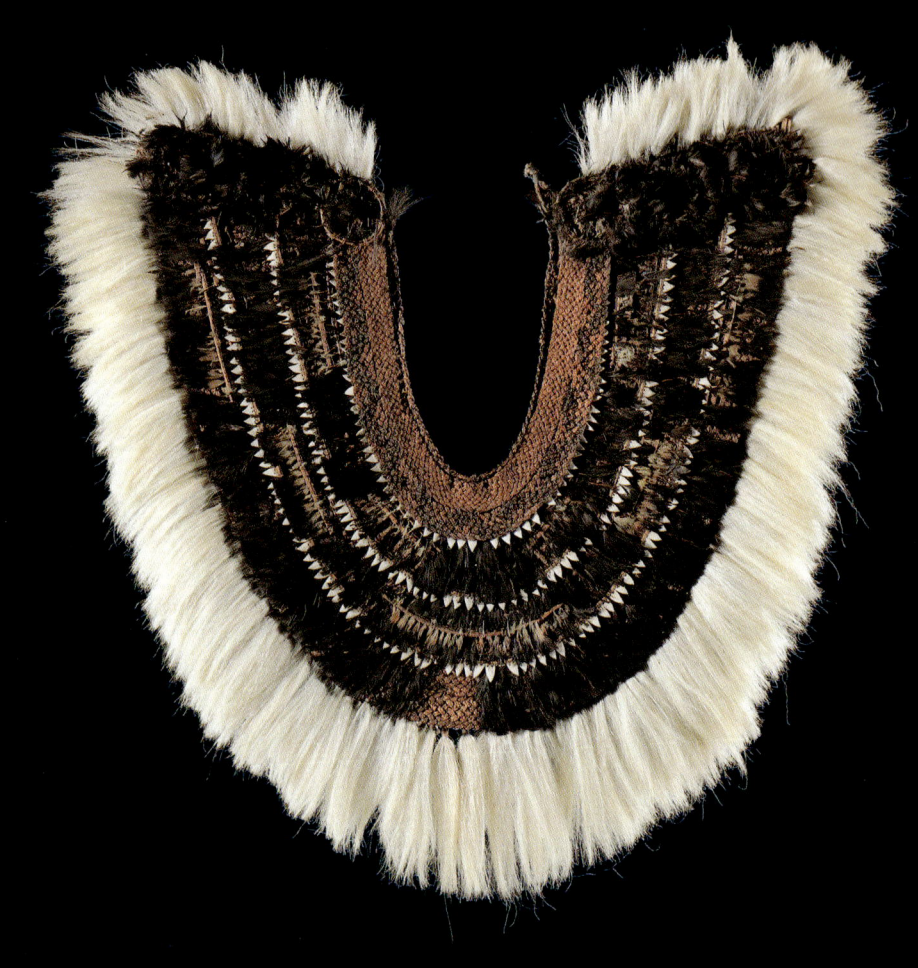

Tāumi (neck armour)

Warfare in the Society Islands often took the form of naval engagements between large double canoes captained by elaborately armoured tribal chiefs. William Hodges, an artist on James Cook's second voyage, witnessed and depicted such impressive scenes.

In battle, the chiefs and their principal lieutenants wore tāumi. This example is an elaborate construction, with a base of woven coconut fibre to which are attached sharks' teeth, feathers, and a fringe of white dog hair. Although tāumi were mostly worn on the breast, a man might occasionally wear two: on the back and on the front, joined at each shoulder.

This tāumi was collected on one of Cook's voyages and is part of the significant holdings that Te Papa has from those expeditions. It was listed in the first catalogue of William Bullock's Museum in 1801, and Charles Winn bought it for £1 2s when the museum was sold in 1819.

Tāumi (neck armour)
late 18th century
Society Islands
Coconut fibre, shark teeth, feathers, dog hair
660 x 670 mm
Gift of Lord St Oswald, 1912

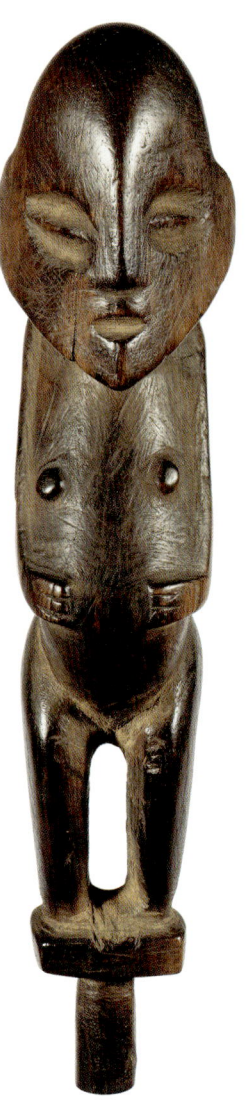

Female deity

This small female figure, a miniature masterpiece of Polynesian carving, is thought to be a deity. It is made from a very hard wood and is attached to a slender, tapering shaft, flattened and perforated at the base. This suggests that it may have been the handle of a sacred fly whisk, similar to known examples from the Society Islands, though W. O. Oldman, the London collector and dealer, recorded that it came from the southern Cook Islands.

The sculpture was probably brought to England in 1823 by George Bennett, who was working in the islands at that time for the London Missionary Society. It later came into the collection of the Duke of Leeds.

During the 1820s, numerous 'idols' from the Cook Islands fell into missionary hands. Many of those illustrated and described by the missionary William Ellis in 1829 were, like this little image, subsequently acquired by Oldman.

Female deity (detail)
early 19th century
Cook Islands or Society Islands
Wood
Carving: 350 x 32 x 32 mm
figure 130 mm length
Purchased 1948, as part of the
Oldman Collection

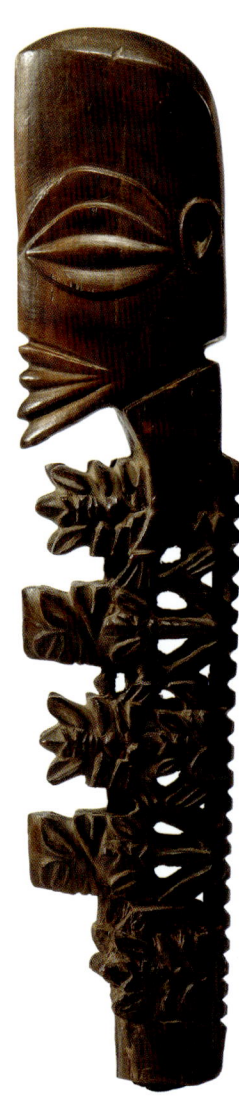

Staff god

Staff gods from Rarotonga consisted of a long wooden staff with an elaborately carved top and a lesser amount of carving at the base. The central shaft was left uncarved and was swathed in a large bundle of tapa (bark cloth).

Missionaries reported seeing 'idols' of this kind up to six metres long, although the largest surviving intact examples are only about one-third that length. This carving is a fine example of an upper section, which has been cut from its shaft. It features a typically smooth head with stylised eyes, mouth, and ears; a curved neck with notches on the back sides; and alternating single and double miniature figures, repetition that is characteristic of Cook Islands carving.

Many staff gods were destroyed when the people of Rarotonga embraced Christianity. Missionaries collected some, along with other religious sculptures, as examples of what missionary Williams Ellis described as the 'imbecility, absurdity, and degradation' of 'idolatry'.

Part of a staff god
early 19th century
Rarotonga, Cook Islands
Wood
600 x 120 mm
Purchased 1948, as part of
the Oldman Collection

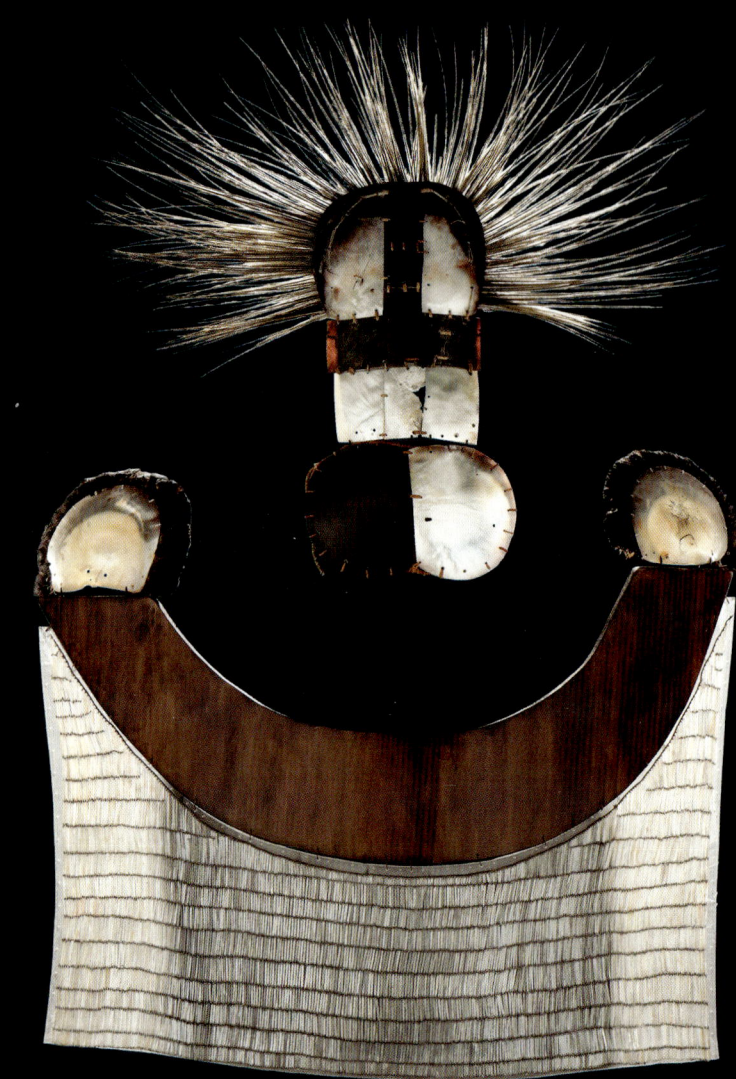

Chief mourner's costume

This mask and chest apron are part of the costume worn by the chief mourner in a Society Islands ritual that fascinated the European observers on Cook's Pacific voyages. On the first voyage, Joseph Banks took part in a ceremony, which was recorded by the visitors in both writings and drawings.

The chief mourner was completely concealed by his elaborate costume. His attendants (including Banks, for a day) wore only loin cloths, and blackened their skins with charcoal and water. The group ranged through the district, making loud noises and terrorising anyone they encountered. This mourning ritual could continue for weeks or months, depending on the ability of the bereaved to feed and pay the mourners.

The costume itself was extremely valuable. Each pearl shell in the mask and apron might have been purchased with a pig, and long hours of labour went into shaping and stitching the many thin shell rectangles in the apron.

Parae (mask) and chest apron, part of mourning costume
late 18th century
Society Islands
Pearl shell, plant fibre, feathers
Mask: 825 x 660 x 80 mm
apron: 910 x 560 mm
Gift of Lord St Oswald, 1912

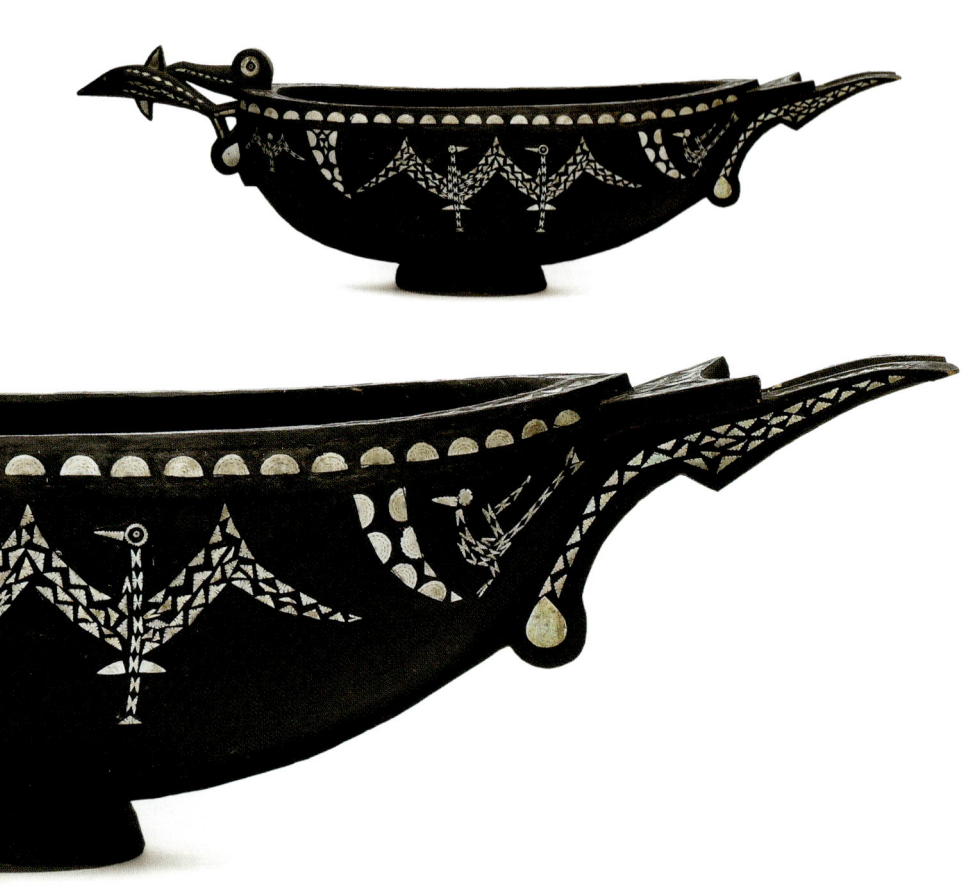

Ceremonial bowl

This large, elaborate bowl is a magnificent example of the art of carvers from the islands of the south-east Solomons. The wooden bowls from the area come in many sizes and shapes, but all are made from the same light wood, stained black with plant juice mixed with charcoal. Most are oval with handles at each end.

Nautilus shells were usually chosen for the inlay on smaller bowls, and cone shells for the larger items. One of the criteria by which a master carver was recognised was his skill in cutting and placing the shell pieces.

The handles are stylised depictions of creatures such as birds, squid, or crickets. Bowls in the form of a bird, with the bird's beak impaling or swallowing a fish, as here, are another variant. This example is thought to have been purchased from the missionary scholar W. G. Ivens in 1909.

Ceremonial bowl
early 20th century
Solomon Islands
Wood, shell
1950 x 450 x 570 mm
Acquisition history unknown

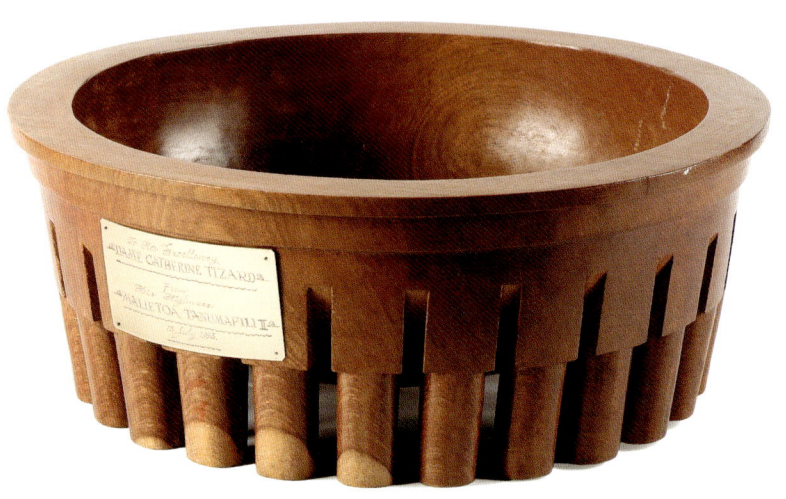

Tānoa faiʻava (kava bowl)

Tānoa faiʻava are wooden bowls used to prepare kava, a beverage made from the roots of the kava plant. The roots are crushed into a powder and mixed in the bowl with water. Kava (or ʻava, as it is known in Samoa) may be served informally, but its most important use is in chiefly meetings and ceremonies.

Historically, the manufacture of tānoa was a specialised task, and certain villages acquired a reputation for producing high-quality work. Older forms of tānoa faiʻava have four legs, whereas most recent examples have many, either round or square, usually set very close together. The bowls can be big enough to serve large formal gatherings or small enough to be portable.

The tānoa faiʻava is an enduring symbol of Samoan hospitality and culture. In 1993, this bowl was presented to the Governor-General of New Zealand, Dame Catherine Tizard, by Western Samoa's head of state, his Highness Malietoa Tanumafili II.

Tānoa faiʻava (kava bowl)
1990s
Samoa
Wood, silver
200 mm height, 505 mm diameter
Gift of Dame Catherine Tizard, 1996

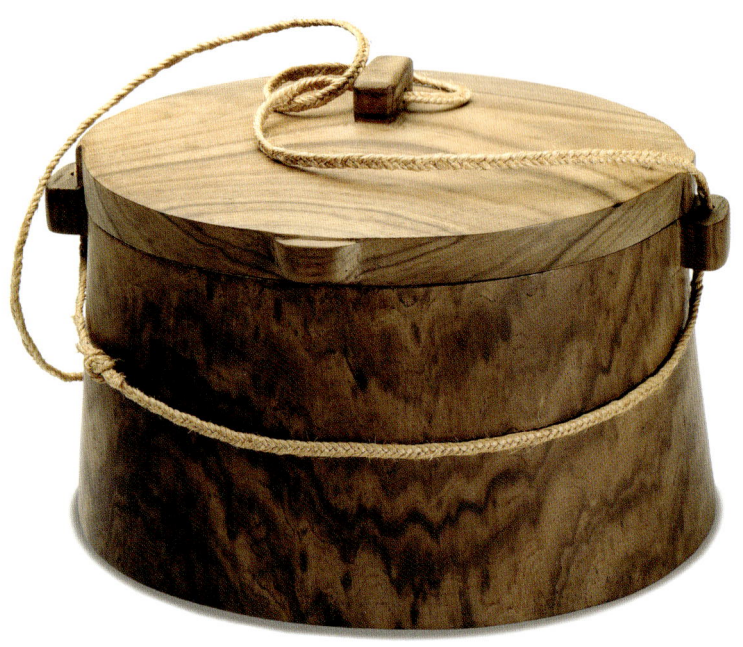

Tuluma (fishing box)

Tuluma are used in Tokelau to carry fishing gear in canoes, or as storage containers at home. A coconut fibre cord keeps the tightly fitting lid lashed down, should the box be dropped or toppled. Tuluma can be very small, or substantial.

Pacific scholar Robert Langdon suggests that Hawaiian castaways wrecked off a Tokelauan atoll around 1830 may have introduced the art of tuluma making: beautifully crafted boxes with fitting lids were seen in Hawai'i from the late 1790s. However, similar boxes are found in other Polynesian islands, such as those in the Tuvalu group, and in parts of Micronesia.

In New Zealand, tuluma usually serve as ornaments or storage containers. This example was made by Elia Tinielu, a member of a Tokelauan community group based in Porirua that has strong ties to the village of Atafu. Atafu people brought the timber and coconut fibre for the tuluma from Tokelau.

Tuluma (fishing box)
1995
Made by Elia Tinielu, New Zealand/ Tokelau
Wood and coconut fibre
185 x 315 x 275 mm
Purchased 1995

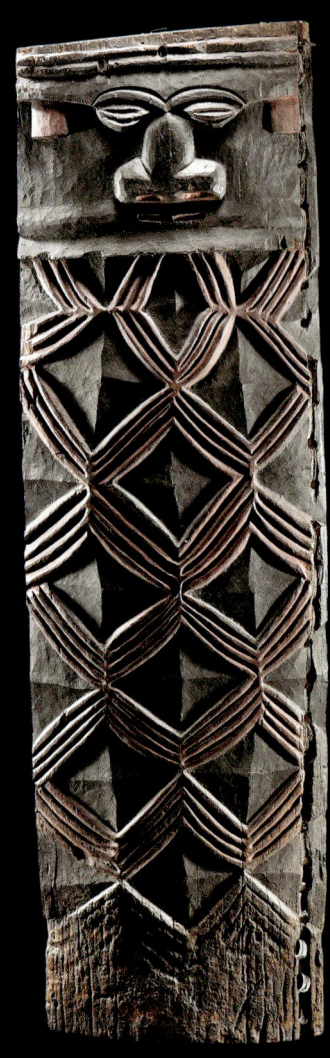

JOVO (house carving)

The great round houses of New Caledonia and the Loyalty Islands were, and still are, powerful symbols of Kanak society. They are used as meeting houses, and reflect social organisation and the relationship between the clans and their chief.

The doorway – with its lintel, sill, and side carvings – was a central focus for architectural sculpture. The large carved boards that flanked the door are among the most striking works of Kanak art. They held in place the horizontal rods that supported the material of the walls. Each great house had two of these carved boards (sometimes known as jovo), although they were seldom an exact pair.

Great houses were found throughout New Caledonia, and there was some regional variation in sculptural styles. Generally, though, the door carvings consisted of an upper face with geometric designs beneath, as here; in the southern region, there might be more than one face.

Jovo (house carving)
late 19th or early 20th century
New Caledonia
Wood
1980 x 540 mm
Purchased 1948, as part of the Oldman Collection

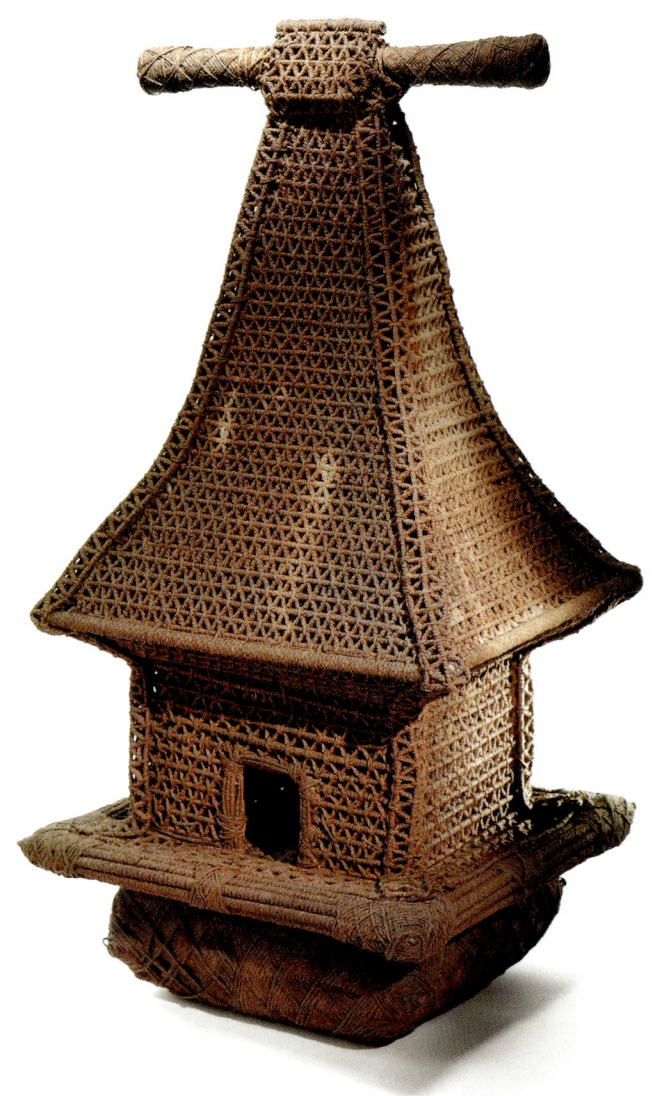

Model burekalou
(spirit house)

Burekalou or spirit houses had a special position in Fijian villages in pre-Christian times. They were the houses of the priests, who were regarded as the mouthpieces of the gods.

The burekalou was usually the grandest dwelling in the Fijian village, in many cases even bigger than the chief's house. It was often built on top of a mound: the higher it stood, or the higher its roof, the closer it took the priests and their prayers to the gods.

When they travelled, priests often took spirit house images with them. This ensured that the spirits could remain within their own abode and in the presence of the priests, who were the only people they trusted to provide for them.

Craftsmen known as the Mataisau (carpenters' clan) were trained to make these model spirit houses. This intricately woven example, with its fine ridgecap and ridgepole, sits on a solid cushion of coconut-fibre cords.

Model burekalou (spirit house)
19th century
Fiji
Wood, coconut fibre
860 mm height; platform: 420 x 410 mm
Acquisition history unknown

33

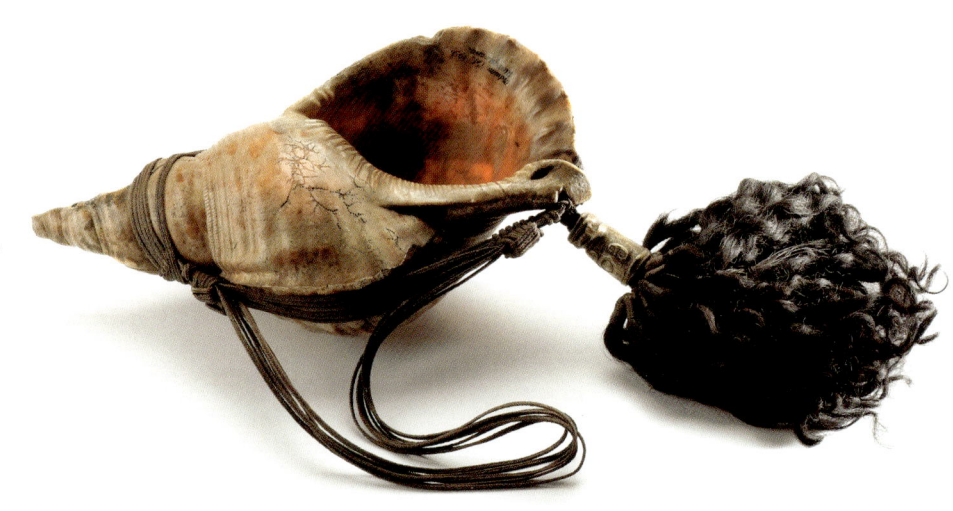

Putona (shell trumpet)

Shell trumpets are used throughout Polynesia and in Fiji, mainly for signalling and for summoning people together. *Charonia tritonis* is the shell preferred, as here, although other shells are sometimes used.

Shell trumpets may be blown from a hole at the end or on the side. This Marquesan putona, old and worn smooth by much handling, was blown from the side. Extremely fine plaited cords of coconut fibre provide lashings and a carrying strap. Tufts of human hair are drawn together in a carved bone toggle and attached to the lashing. The toggle, carved in a tiki (human figure) form, is characteristic of Marquesan art. In the Marquesas, decorated trumpets such as this were used in times of war.

Māori in New Zealand made pūtātara, fitted with a wooden mouthpiece, using a smaller local shell until large tropical shells began appearing as trade items in the nineteenth century.

Putona (shell trumpet)
19th century
Marquesas Islands, French Polynesia
Shell, coconut fibre, human hair, bone
350 mm length; hair tuft: *c.* 200 mm
Purchased 1948, as part of
the Oldman Collection

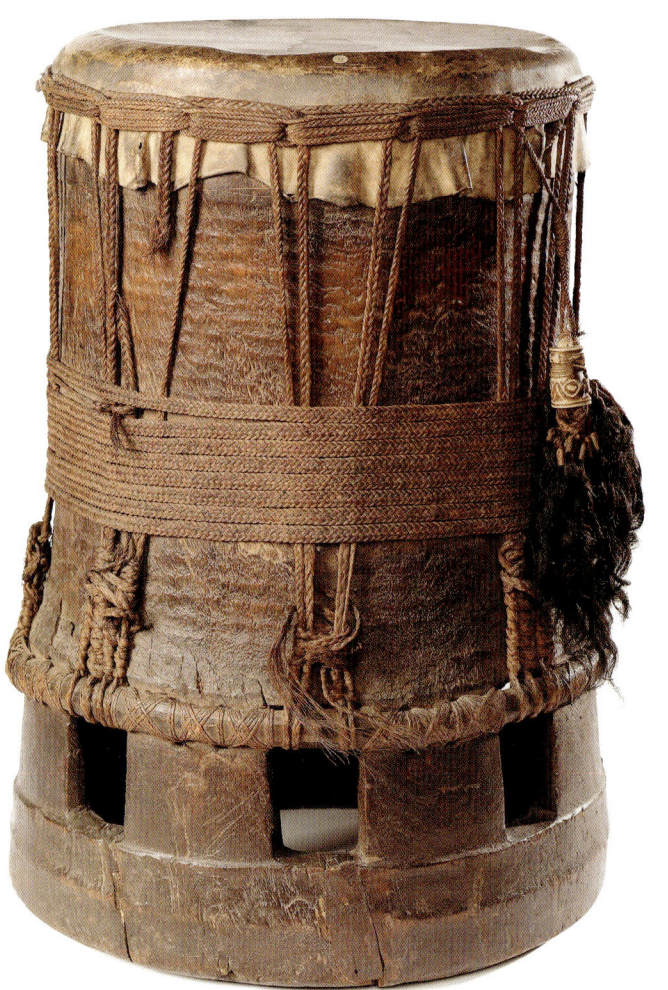

Taitai or pahu (drum)

Single-skin, footed drums called taitai or pahu were a feature of several eastern Polynesian island groups. In Hawai'i and parts of French Polynesia, including the Marquesas, they were used in elaborate religious rituals, accompanying song and dance or signalling various stages of the ceremony.

Such drums were works of art. Those from Hawai'i and Austral Island sometimes had ornate carving on the wooden body, with fine plain lashings. Drums from the Marquesas were decorated with very detailed plaiting and attached ornaments, as with this drum's cord-covered wooden hoop and delicately carved bone toggle in tiki (human figure) form.

The drum has been hollowed from each end, leaving a solid septum or partition between the resonating chamber and the base. The shark-skin membrane is secured by coconut fibre cords fastened to a wooden hoop, which is lashed to the body of the drum. It stood on the ground when played.

Taitai or pahu (drum)
19th century
Marquesas Islands
Wood, shark skin, coconut fibre, hair, bone
660 mm height, 455 mm diameter
Purchased 1948, as part of the Oldman Collection

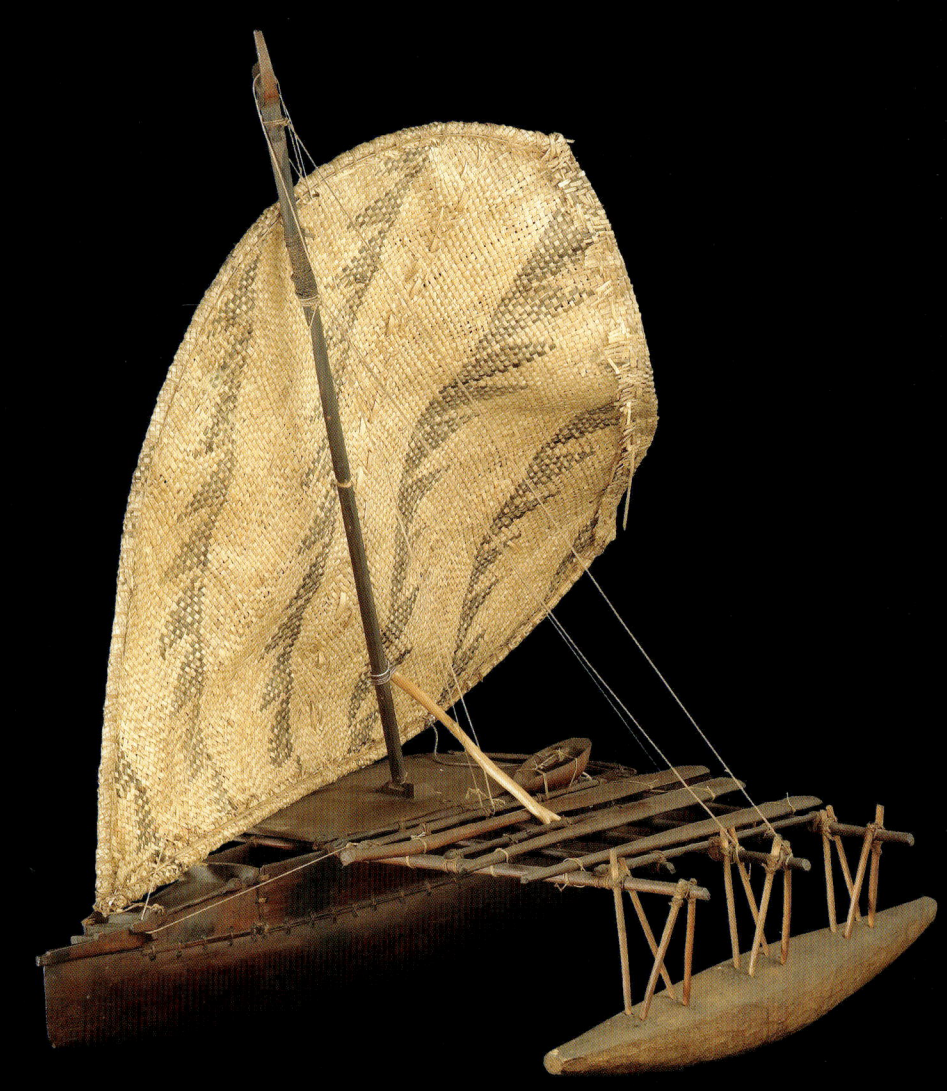

Model camakau
(outrigger sailing canoe)

Camakau were fast, highly manoeuvrable outrigger canoes used to travel among the Fijian islands. Their average length was 12 metres, although some were as long as 30 metres. The hulls were made from a single tree trunk or two trunks joined together; sails were made from pandanus mats.

A larger canoe required a crew of forty to handle the heavy triangular sail and rigging. Eyewitnesses frequently noted the dexterity with which these camakau were handled. A well-drilled crew could manoeuvre the sail and mast so expertly that the vessel would be on a new tack within 60 seconds.

Models of canoes and other sailing vessels have long been popular with collectors. As tourism has grown, so too has the demand for models, along with a decline in the standards of workmanship. Models from the nineteenth century are often highly detailed, and provide a fascinating insight into this disappearing maritime tradition.

Model of a camakau
(large outrigger sailing canoe)
19th century
Fiji
Wood, fibre, pandanus
910 x 470 x 750 mm
Acquisition history unknown

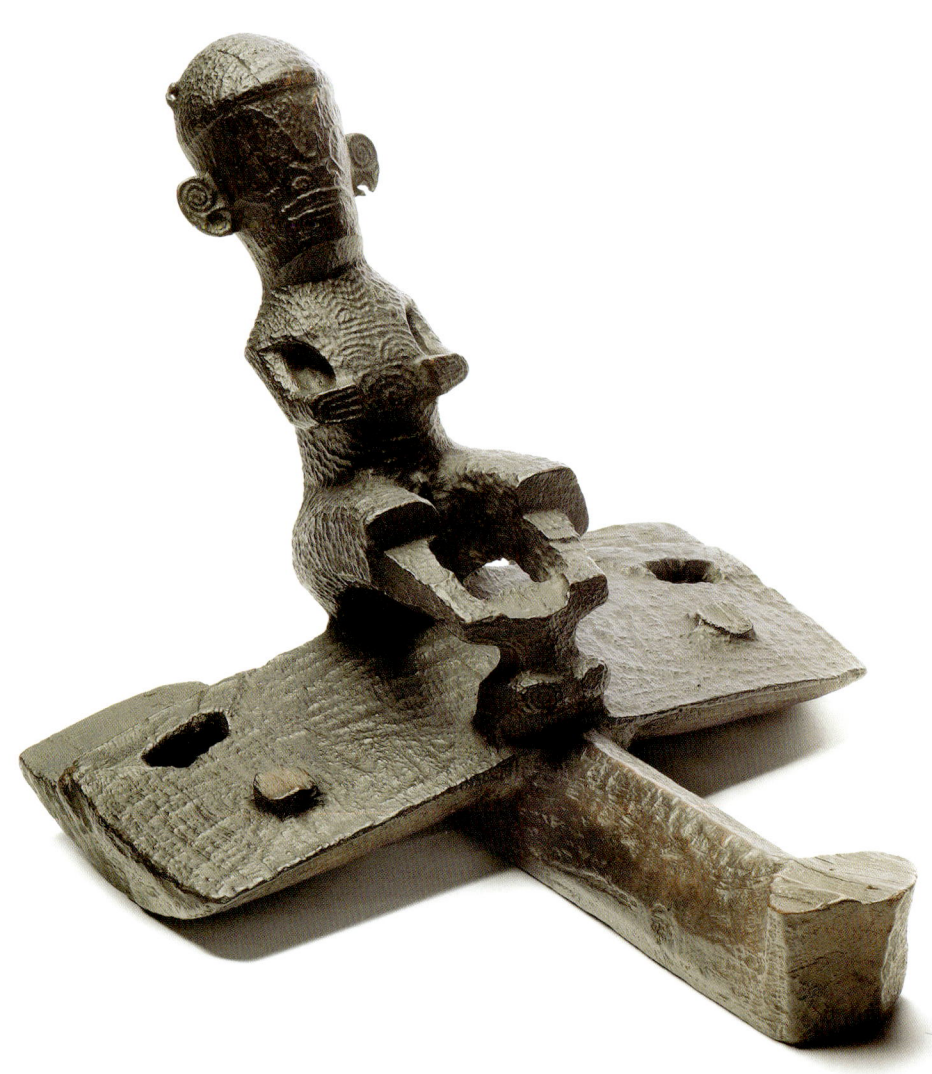

Canoe figure

Marquesan art is often compared to Māori because of its sculptural use of the human figure and extensive decorative carving. This small sculpture, thought to be a canoe prow carving, is similar to the figure at the base of a Māori taurapa (stern post). It may have represented a deity associated with the sea, perhaps with fishing.

The principal figure is male, his legs held up by a smaller facing figure whose head is now missing. The fine surface carving covering them represents the full body tattoo of a Marquesan man. On the back of the complete figure's head are two pierced lugs, which could have held strings of feathers or other types of decoration.

The Marquesan tiki (human) figure appears in many forms – in large stone images of deities and wooden house-posts, stone figurines used in rituals, and bone toggles. Small three-dimensional wooden images are rare; most are found on canoe carvings.

Canoe figure
19th century
Marquesas Islands
Wood
375 x 260 x 220 mm
Purchased 1948, as part of
the Oldman Collection

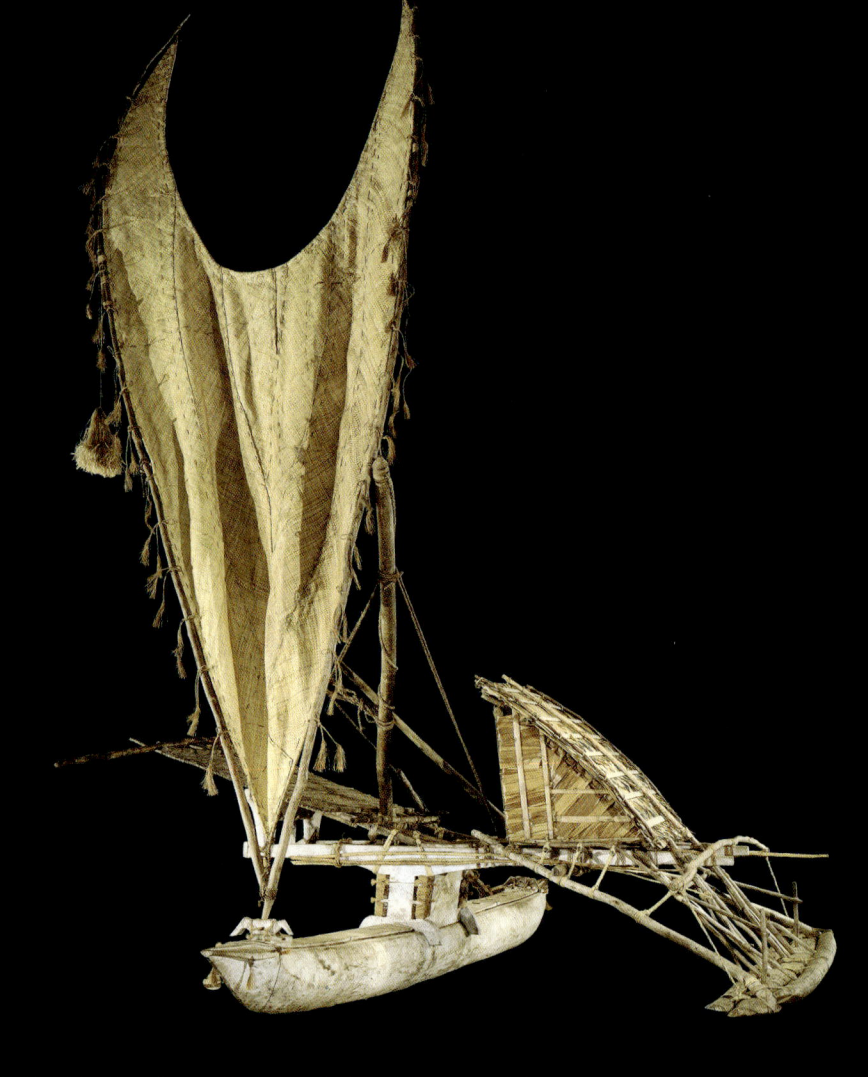

Parangaina

Tepuke (sailing canoes) were once common in the Temotu province of the Solomon Islands. Up to 20 metres long, they were used to carry people and goods along trading routes and between the region's many small island communities.

New forms of sea transport in the late twentieth century saw a marked decline in their use. The ensuing loss of knowledge about building and sailing tepuke was a concern to many local people, including William Keizy, a former policeman. After consulting with family and community elders, he undertook to construct this tepuke. It was named *Parangaina* – 'impossibility' – because no one believed he could do it.

Parangaina is seven metres long. Its huge, crab claw-like sail is made from pandanus-leaf mats, carefully stitched together. A small shelter on the deck keeps cargo and provisions dry during sea voyages. Its launch in 1997 coincided with other local initiatives aimed at recovering knowledge about these craft.

Parangaina, tepuke (sailing canoe)
1997
Made by William Keizy, Taumako, Solomon Islands
Wood, pandanus, coconut fibre, cane
6800 mm length
decking: 4270 mm width
Purchased 1997 with New Zealand Lottery Grants Board funds

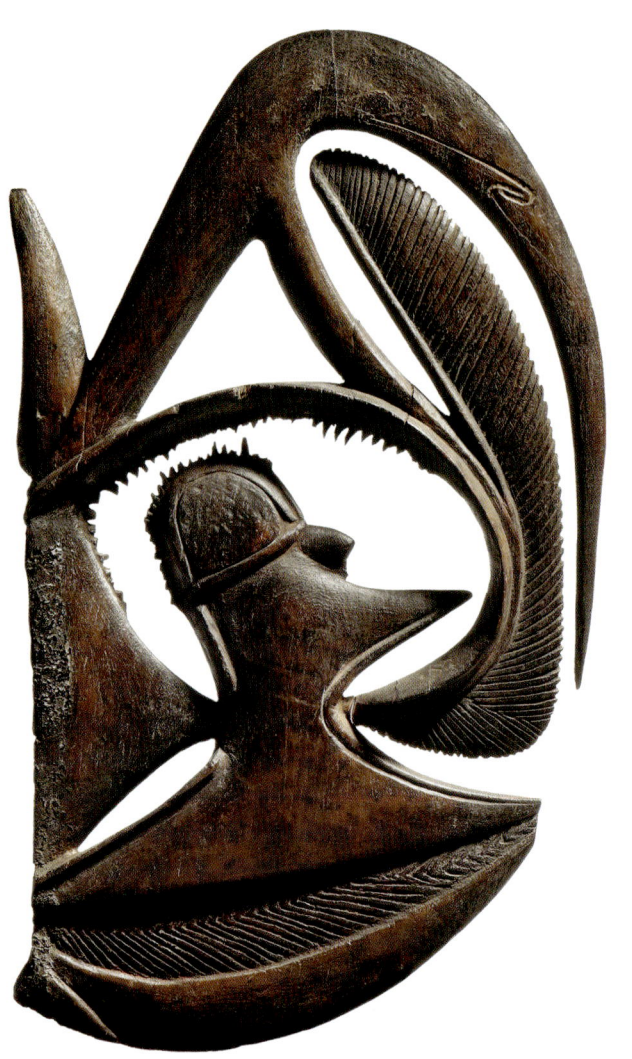

Canoe carving

This unique and enigmatic sculpture is one of the treasures of the Oldman Collection. It is generally thought to be a canoe carving, which Oldman attributed to Kaniet, a small island north of the Admiralty Islands in Papua New Guinea.

Even the correct orientation of this sculpture is in doubt. It is usually depicted, as here, with what appears to be a central human head facing slightly upwards. When it is rotated 90 degrees, a shape that might be a seabird becomes more prominent. There is a groove along one edge, which has apparently enabled the carving to be glued or lashed to another piece of wood. This would support Oldman's theory that it was part of a canoe prow.

Few examples of Kaniet art from this era survive. Other evidence for the carving's origin is mainly circumstantial – Kaniet's ocean-bound position, its people's strong canoe-building traditions, and their cultural affiliations with the sea-going peoples of Micronesia.

Canoe carving
19th century
Kaniet, Papua New Guinea
Wood
465 x 295 mm
Purchased 1948, as part of the Oldman Collection

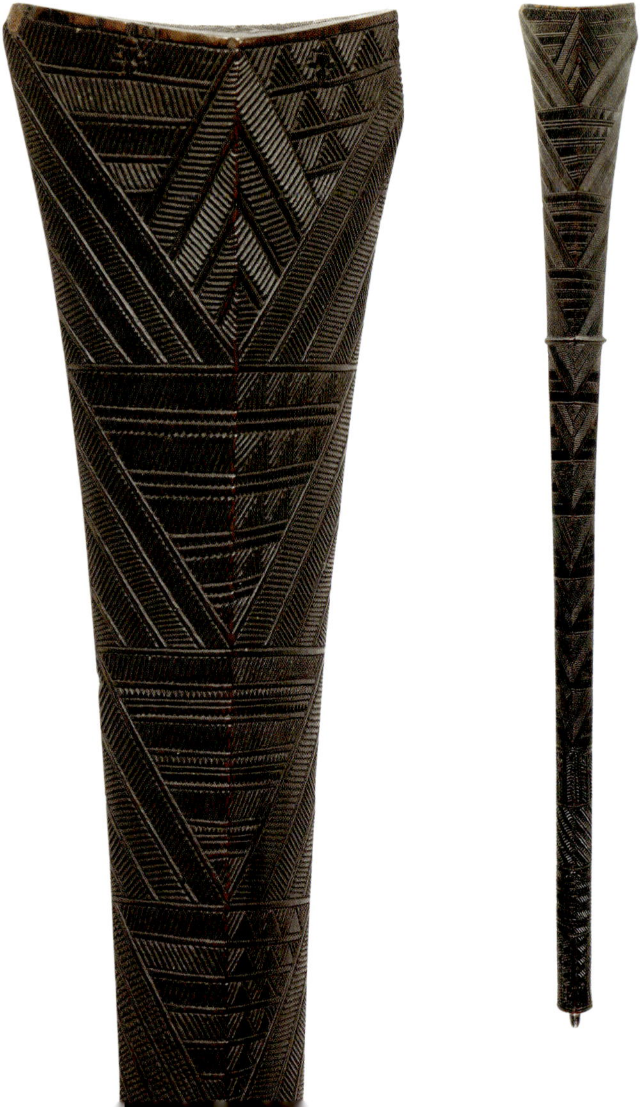

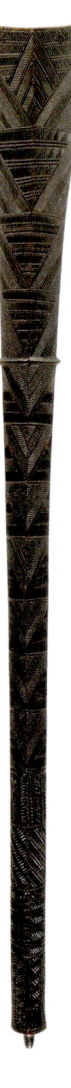

Club

Fighting clubs were the principal
weapons of Tonga, Samoa, and Fiji.
Similar in length to Māori taiaha (fighting
staffs), they were often splendidly carved.
Tongan clubs, in particular, are renowned
for their geometric patterns and miniature
figures, which were shown engaged in
male activities such as hunting, fishing,
pigeon snaring, and fighting.

This club is thought to have been
collected on James Cook's second or
third voyage. It is completely covered with
incised decoration, including several tiny
figures on the shaft and the flattened top.
Most of the carving is extremely fine, and
was probably executed with a shark-tooth
implement. The coarser carving in the
handle area (the tapered end) probably
helped with the weapon's grip, but may
also indicate the use of a nail or other
metal tool.

The carving of such clubs took place over
a long period – sometimes years. But this
work-in-progress would still be used as a
weapon throughout.

Club
18th century
Tonga
Wood
930 x 104 mm
Gift of Lord St Oswald, 1912

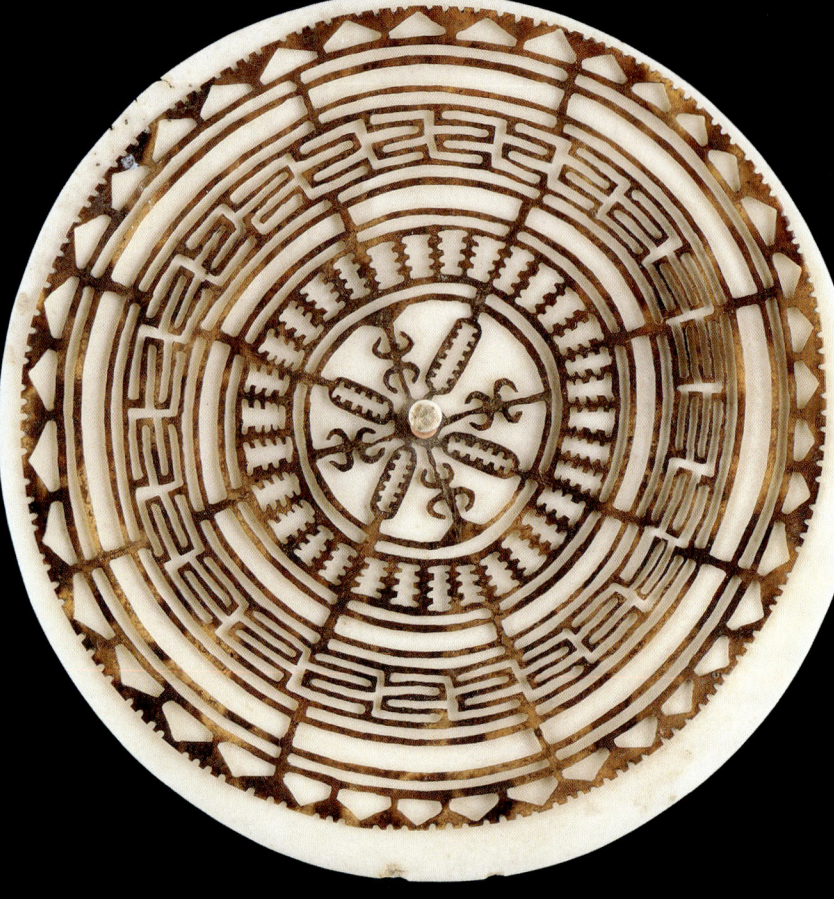

Kapkap
(forehead or shoulder ornament)

Kapkaps, as ornaments like this are now called, are found in parts of Papua New Guinea and the Solomon Islands. These skilfully made shell disks are overlaid with delicate turtle-shell filigree. Worn on the forehead, breast, or shoulder, they are much admired. A similar ornament (for the forehead) occurs far to the east in the Marquesas Islands.

The shell disk was usually made from giant clam shell, the cutting of which is a laborious task. More easily worked shells were used in the Papuan Gulf; in the Marquesas, the disk might be pearl shell. In recent times, brown plastic has been used for the overlay.

Archaeological evidence from Temotu Province in the Solomons shows that people there have been wearing shell disks for more than two thousand years. The overlays may have developed much more recently.

Kapkap
(forehead or shoulder ornament)
late 19th century
Solomon Islands
Shell, turtle shell, plant fibre
117 mm diameter
Purchased 1914

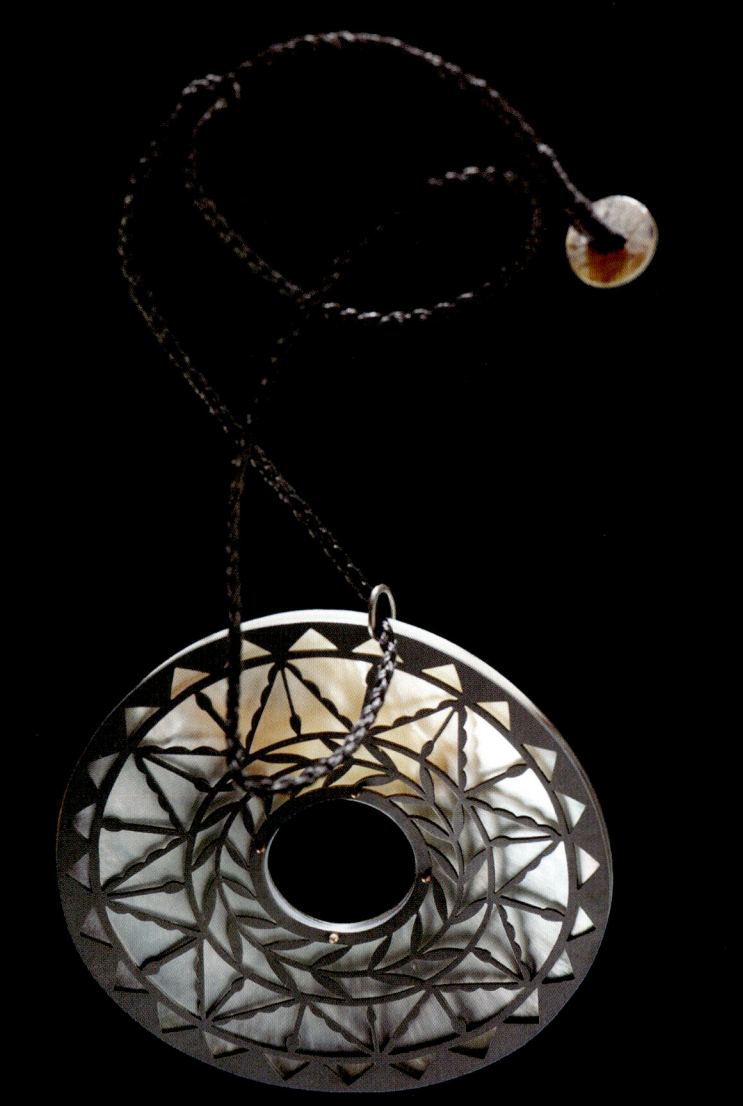

Niki Hastings-McFall

Niki Hastings-McFall is one of a small group of artists who explore Pacific aspects of their multicultural heritage through contemporary jewellery. Using a variety of materials, both natural and synthetic, found and made, she draws on both her Samoan ancestry and her contemporary New Zealand experience.

Hastings-McFall began exhibiting in 1992. Her early pieces reflected a deep connection with the sea. She is fascinated by the history, culture, and art styles of the Pacific, and is increasingly concerned with environmental and political issues.

In *Siapo Mamanu, Stored Knowledge*, the artist combines silver and pearl shell to produce an elegant modern pendant. It makes specific reference to the kapkap (page 48) and the civavonovono (page 60). Hastings-McFall's admiration for the work of the old craftspeople, especially their mastery of materials, is clear. In 'copying' their work, although in different materials, she seems almost to participate in the workshops of the original makers.

Niki Hastings-McFall
(born 1959), Samoa/New Zealand
Siapo Mamanu, Stored Knowledge
2000
Patinated silver, pearl shell, linen cord
95 mm diameter
Purchased 2001

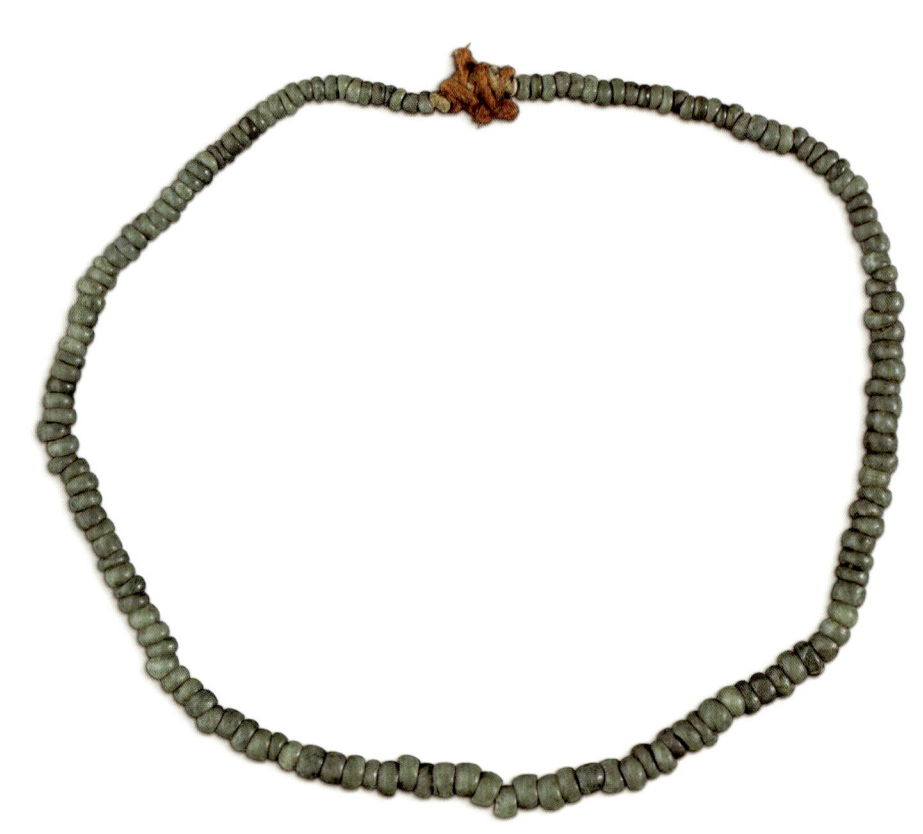

Meciwe (necklace)

Like New Zealand, the main island of New Caledonia is a fragment of the ancient continent of Gondwanaland. Also like New Zealand, New Caledonia has a form of jade (nephrite) valued for its beauty and its hardness. Just as Māori used pounamu, so the Kanak people used their jade for axe blades – both utilitarian and ceremonial – and for personal adornments.

These adornments took the form of large jade beads, laboriously worked and strung into necklaces, often decorated with red fur from a flying fox. Such necklaces were the exclusive property of the wives of chiefs, and among the most highly valued of Kanak possessions. Visitors to New Caledonia in the first half of the nineteenth century found that women would not part with their necklaces at any price.

This jade necklace is part of a significant group of New Caledonian objects held at Te Papa, most of which came with the Oldman Collection.

Meciwe (necklace)
late 19th or early 20th century
New Caledonia
Jade and plant fibre
340 mm length
Purchased 1948, as part of
the Oldman Collection

53

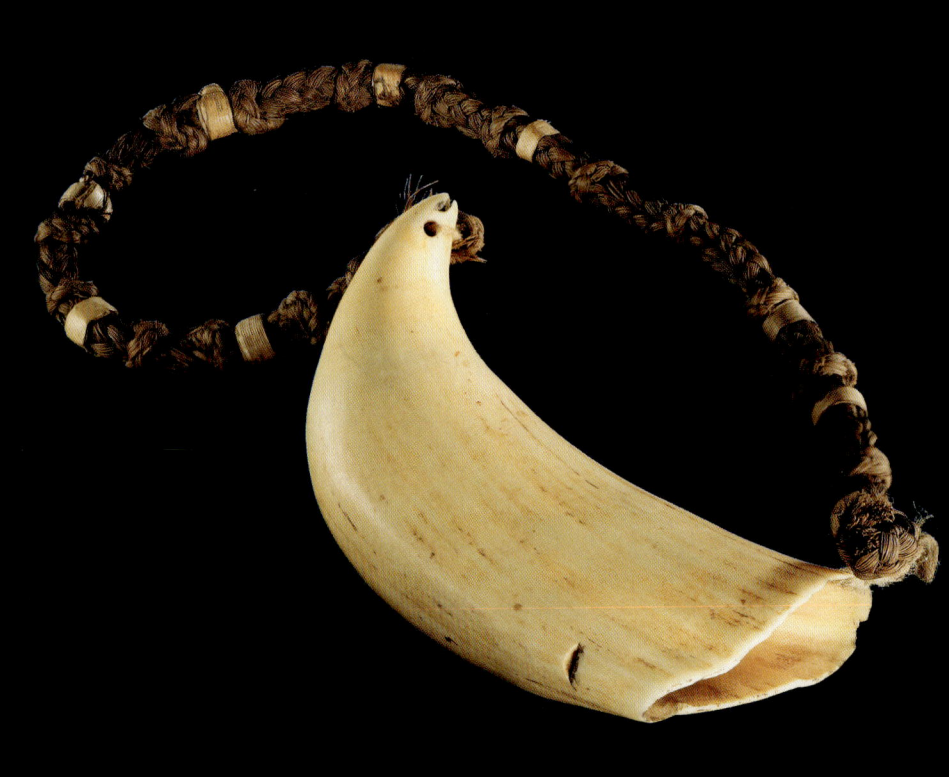

Tabua
(ceremonial whale tooth)

Tabua are an important part of ceremonial custom in Fijian life, playing many cultural and spiritual roles. They might be presented as marriage tokens, as atonement, or when a particular favour is being sought. In such cases, their acceptance is spiritually binding.

Tabua can also signal a negative response. To confirm that a marriage proposal has been rejected, for example, a girl's family must reciprocate with double the number of tabua presented by the prospective groom's family.

Originally, some tabua were carved from wood, but whale teeth were preferred, those from the lower jaw of the sperm whale being especially prized. A large cream-coloured whale tooth has been carefully polished and worked to make this tabua, and the tip and butt pierced to allow a cord to be attached. The cord is a thick, tight plait of sennit (coconut fibre) with ornamental knots and bands of pandanus leaf set at regular intervals.

Tabua (ceremonial whale tooth)
19th century
Fiji
Sperm whale tooth, coconut fibre, pandanus leaf
Tooth: 168 x 70 x 55 mm
Gift of R. L. Holmes, 1887

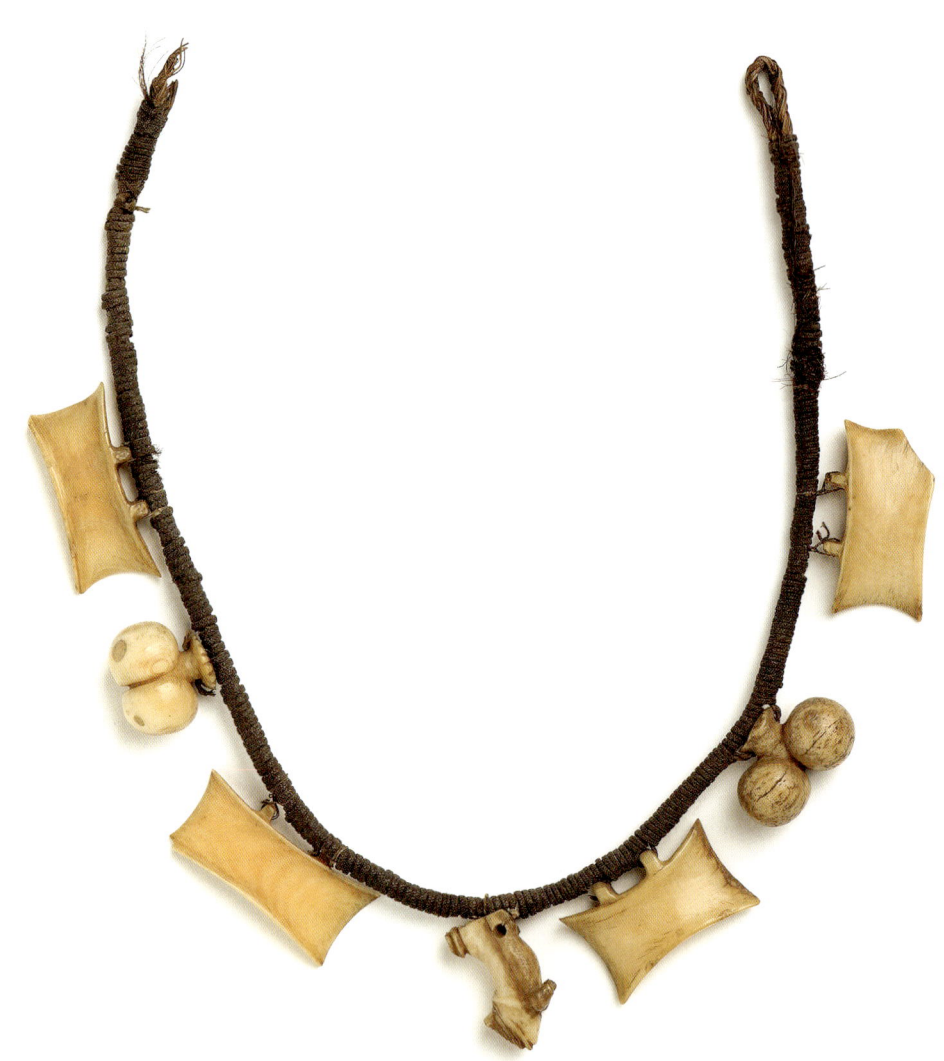

Rei (necklace)

Sea-mammal ivory was prized for personal adornment and for ceremonial presentation in many parts of the Pacific, including New Zealand. At times whole teeth were used; otherwise the ivory was worked into intricate ear ornaments, or beads and small pendants. The latter were strung on fibre to make necklaces.

This ivory and bone necklace is an elegant example, probably from Mangaia in the southern Cook Islands, and worn only by someone of high status. It has a characteristic combination of amulets – concave-edged rectangular tabs of sea-mammal ivory, an animal figure (probably a pig), and a pair of double spheres of ivory or bone. The cord is made of fine coconut fibre and human hair.

Nothing is known about the symbolism of the amulets, though some scholars believe that the double spheres could represent testicles. There are parallels with a small group of early Māori stone amulets of similar shape.

Rei (necklace)
19th century
Mangaia, Cook Islands (attributed)
Sea-mammal ivory, bone, coconut fibre, hair
470 mm length
Purchased 1948, as part of the Oldman Collection

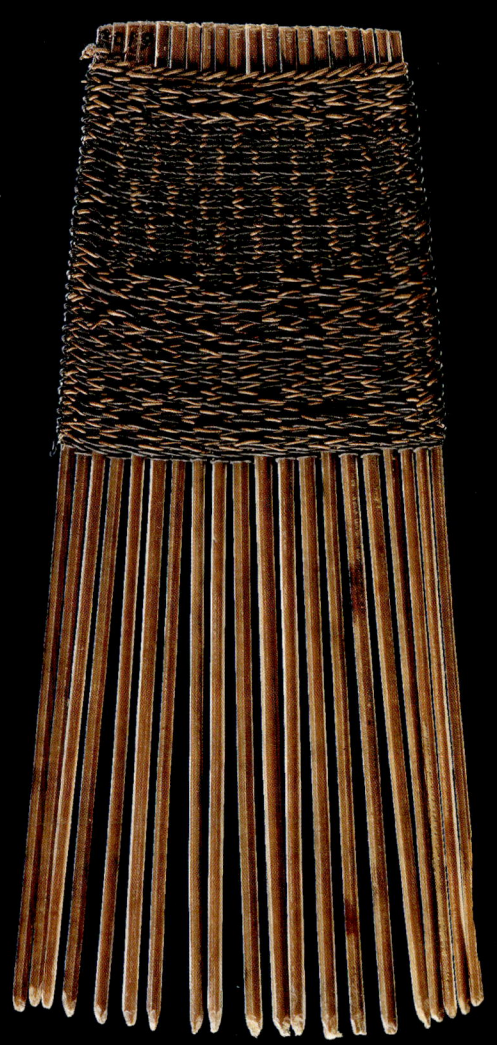

Helu (comb)

William Anderson, the surgeon on James Cook's third voyage, noted that Tongan women made cloth, mats, many varieties of basket, and 'vast numbers' of combs. This classic example of an ornamental comb from Tonga consists of twenty segments of dried coconut-leaf midrib, bound together by a decorative lashing of fine coconut fibre and possibly human hair.

Such combs would be worn projecting upright at the back of the head. They might also be used as beard ornaments, with the decorative handle left protruding. In Tonga, the combs worn by distinguished chiefs were decorated with fine designs and red parrot feathers: such nobles had attendants whose sole responsibility was to look after their hair.

The comb was probably collected during Cook's first visit to the island group in 1773. It is part of a collection once owned by Queen Victoria and given to the Imperial Institute in London by King Edward VII.

Helu (comb)
late 18th century
Tonga
Coconut-leaf midrib, coconut fibre
113 x 52 mm
Gift of the Imperial Institute, 1955

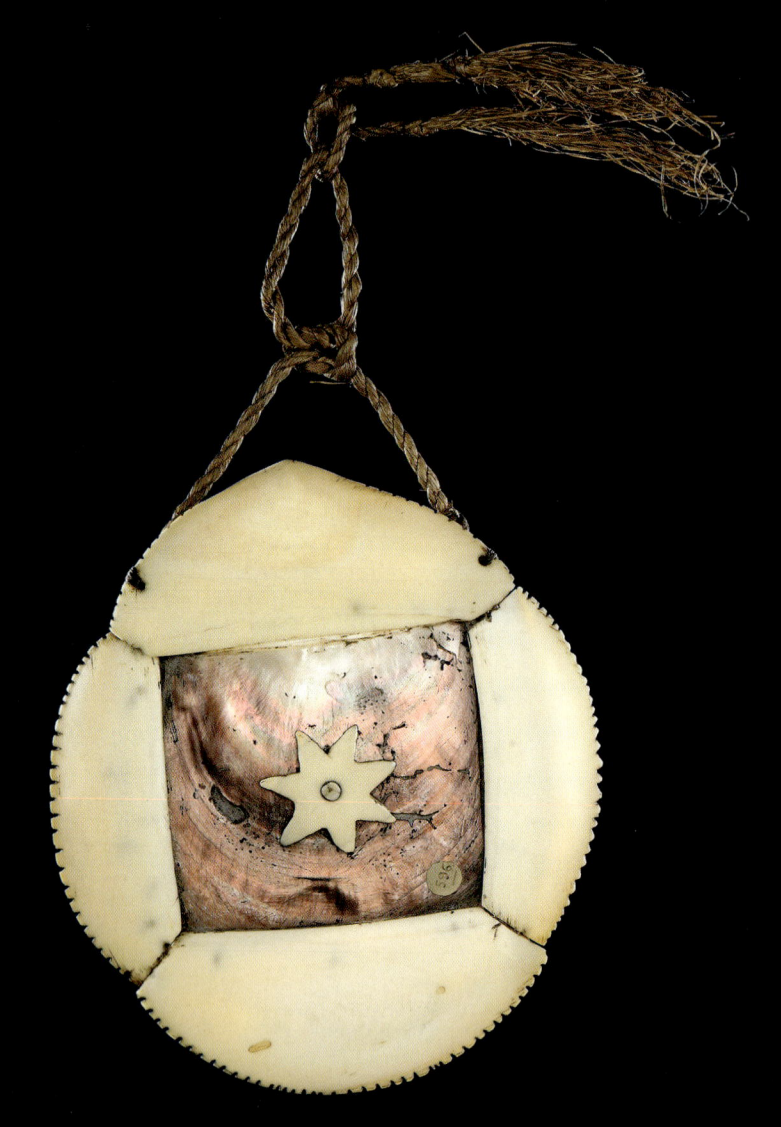

Civavonovono (breastplate)

Pearl-shell breastplates (civa in Fijian) were worn as ornaments by chiefs in Fiji and much of Polynesia. They were highly valued and often used in ceremonial presentations.

In the early nineteenth century, more elaborate styles of civa evolved in Fiji as makers took advantage of the metal tools that were increasingly available, and of the whale teeth supplied by whalers. The civavonovono is a style that has a pearl shell with whale-tooth plates attached to the outside surface. There is often a central whale-tooth star, as in this example. Here, the plates are lashed to the shell with plant fibre, but in many cases they were attached with copper rivets. Another style, civatabua, consists of whale-tooth plates stitched together, sometimes with a central core of pearl shell.

Breastplates like these were believed to make the wearers invulnerable to arrows, and many found their way to warring areas in Fiji as military payments.

Civavonovono (breastplate)
19th century
Fiji
Pearl shell, whale tooth, plant fibre
180 x 155 mm
Purchased 1948, as part of
the Oldman Collection

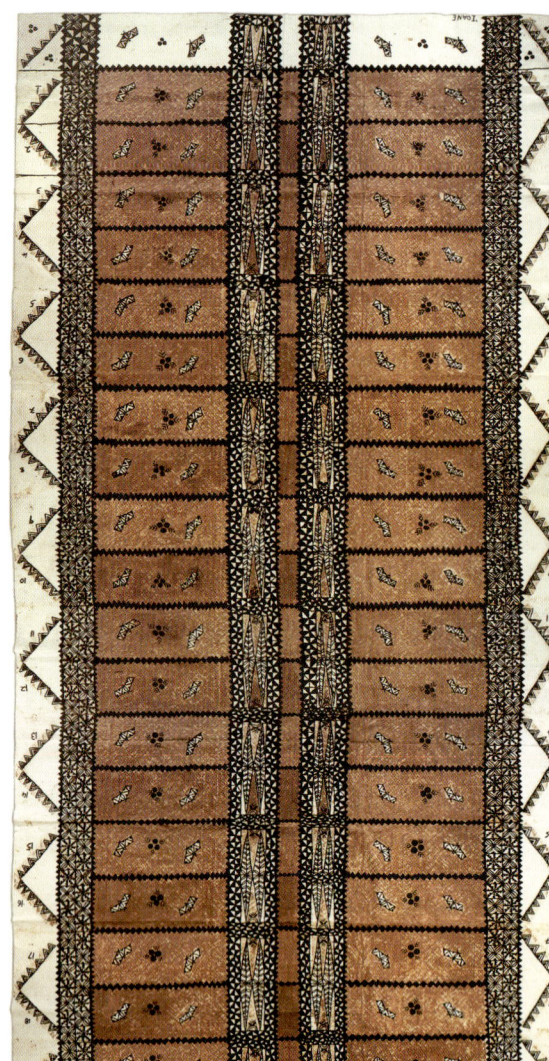

Ngatu tupenu vilene
(decorated bark cloth)

The manufacture of ngatu tupenu vilene is a recent development in the textile arts of Tongan women in New Zealand. Unlike ngatu (bark cloth), which is customarily made from the bark of the paper mulberry plant, these decorated cloths are produced from a synthetic material called Vilene (used as stiffening in clothing).

This ngatu was made by the Ilo Me'a Fo'ou (New Creations) Tongan Women's Group, based in Upper Hutt, north of Wellington. Sections of Vilene were pasted together in the same way as bark cloth to form a very large single piece. It was then hand-decorated in the usual way, using customary Tongan design motifs.

This community group aims to continue the practice of Tongan tapa-making, despite the lack of the usual plant materials in New Zealand. The qualities of Vilene enable the group to make a product that looks like tapa (decorated bark cloth), and can be used in Tongan ceremonial exchange in exactly the same way.

Ngatu tupenu vilene
(decorated bark cloth)
1996
Made by Ilo Me'a Fo'ou (New Creations)
Tongan Women's Group
Vilene (synthetic material), dyes
4.6 x 12.21 m
Purchased 1997 with New Zealand
Lottery Grants Board funds

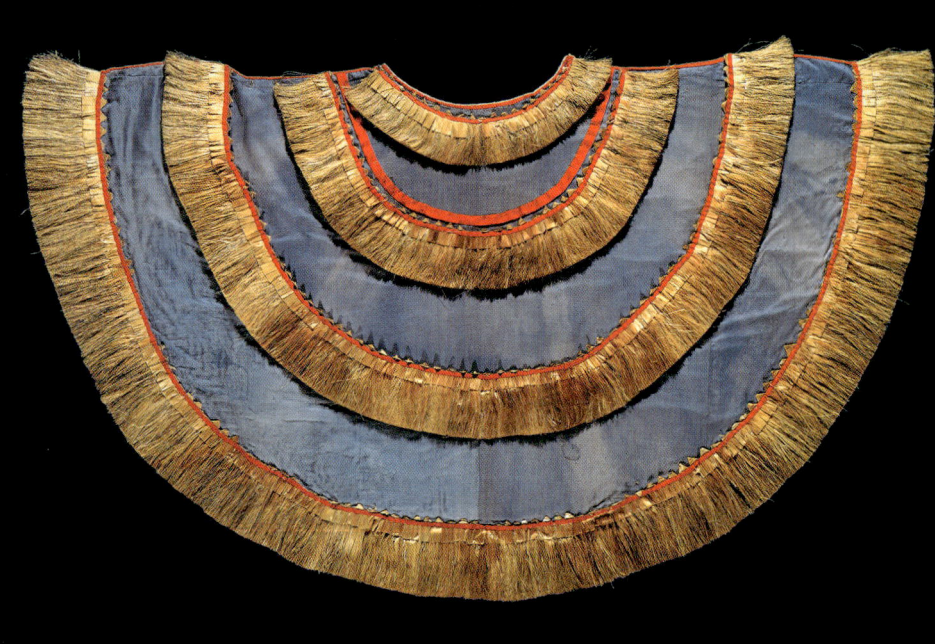

Cloak

In 1872, the Rarotongan chief Te Aia Mataiapo gave this magnificent cloak to the New Zealand government in gratitude for the hospitality he had received during a visit to Auckland.

In pre-European Polynesian societies, people of high rank sometimes wore very fine garments, or large quantities of mats or bark cloth. Decorative, colourful cloaks were found only in New Zealand and Hawai'i. The introduction of European cloth and fashions of dress provided opportunities for new expressions of status throughout the islands. Pacific Islands women began experimenting with different styles and materials, often with striking results.

This cloak demonstrates the way its makers have combined imported fabric and indigenous fibre for clothing or ceremonial dress. The body of the cloak is a very fine blue woollen cloth; the red trim is also imported fabric. The golden fibres are kiri'au (the Cook Islands name for the inner fibre of hibiscus bark).

Cloak
c. 1870
Rarotonga, Cook Islands
Cashmere wool, hibiscus fibre
1390 x 2180 mm
Gift of Te Aia Mataiapo, 1872

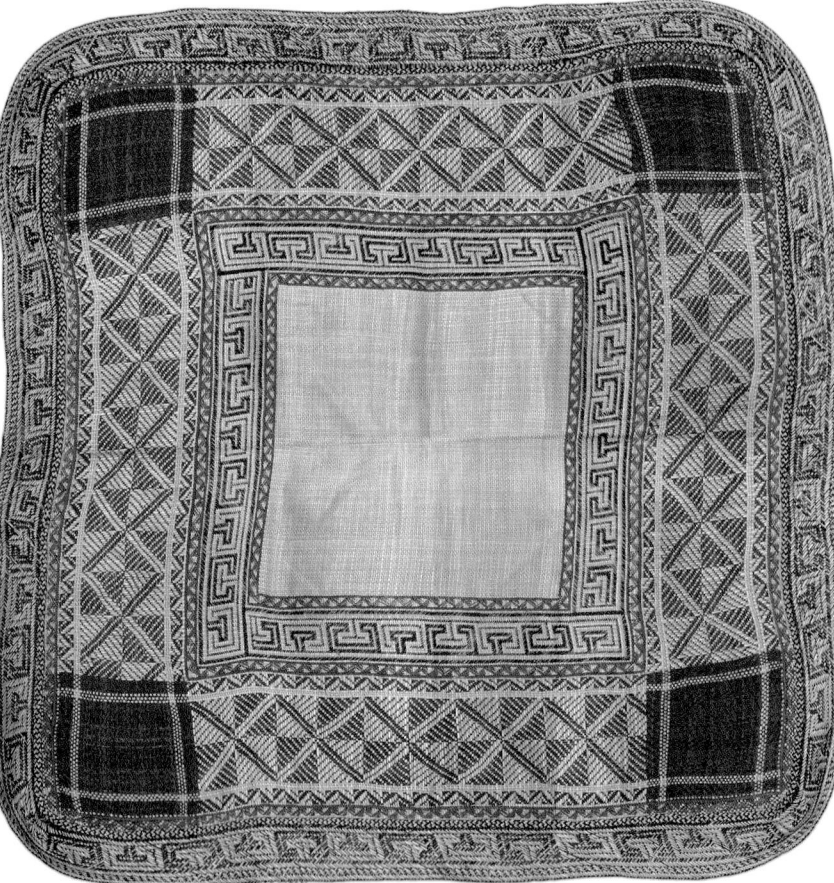

Costume mat, Marshall Islands

The term 'mat' has been used in the Pacific to describe anything from floor coverings through to bedding, articles of dress, and currency. One of the major uses of mats was in clothing, including skirts, loincloths, capes, and head-coverings.

Marshallese costume mats are remarkable for their intricate geometric patterns. As in this example, they were usually constructed from several pieces neatly stitched together. All have a similar pattern of concentric squares with a plain centre, and each mat features several different motifs.

A woman's costume consisted of two quite small mats (usually about 900 millimetres square, as here), not necessarily matching. One was wrapped around the front of the body and the other around the back; the second mat overlapped the first but left a gap in front through which the first could be seen. The skirt was held in place by a girdle, often a string of shells or shell beads.

Costume mat
late 19th or early 20th century
Marshall Islands
Plant fibres
910 x 890 mm
Purchased 1911

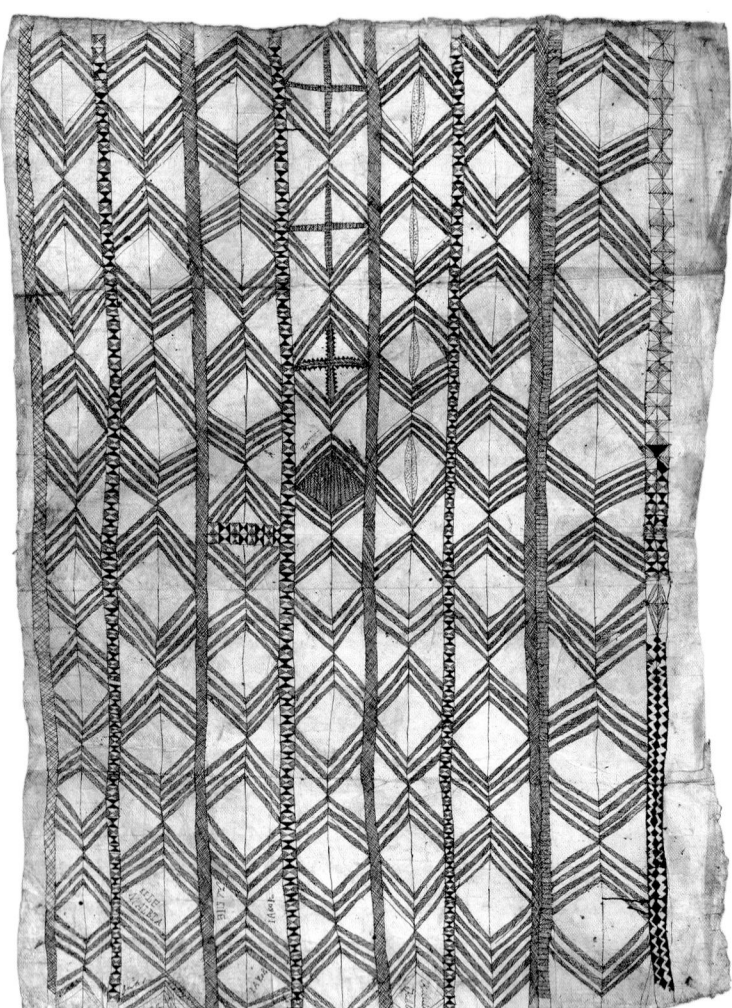

Hiapo (decorated bark cloth)

Hiapo is the name given to decorated bark cloth from the raised atoll of Niue. Little is known about its early forms, but it was probably used for coverings and possibly in gift giving.

Samoan methods of making bark cloth were introduced to Niue in the 1830s by Samoan missionaries. Through the mid-nineteenth century, the patterns and motifs on Niuean hiapo and on Samoan siapo were often indistinguishable. In the 1880s, however, some hiapo makers developed a freehand style of decoration, using a distinctly Niuean iconography, with intricate line-work and detailed motifs based on various species of plants.

Although this hiapo was made before the 1880s, there are several signatures among its crosshatched lines that are typical of the later period. They offer a slender connection not only to the makers of this hiapo but also to an art form that by the early twentieth century had disappeared from Niuean culture.

Hiapo (decorated bark cloth)
c. 1860
Niue
Bark cloth
2000 x 1360 mm
Purchased 1988

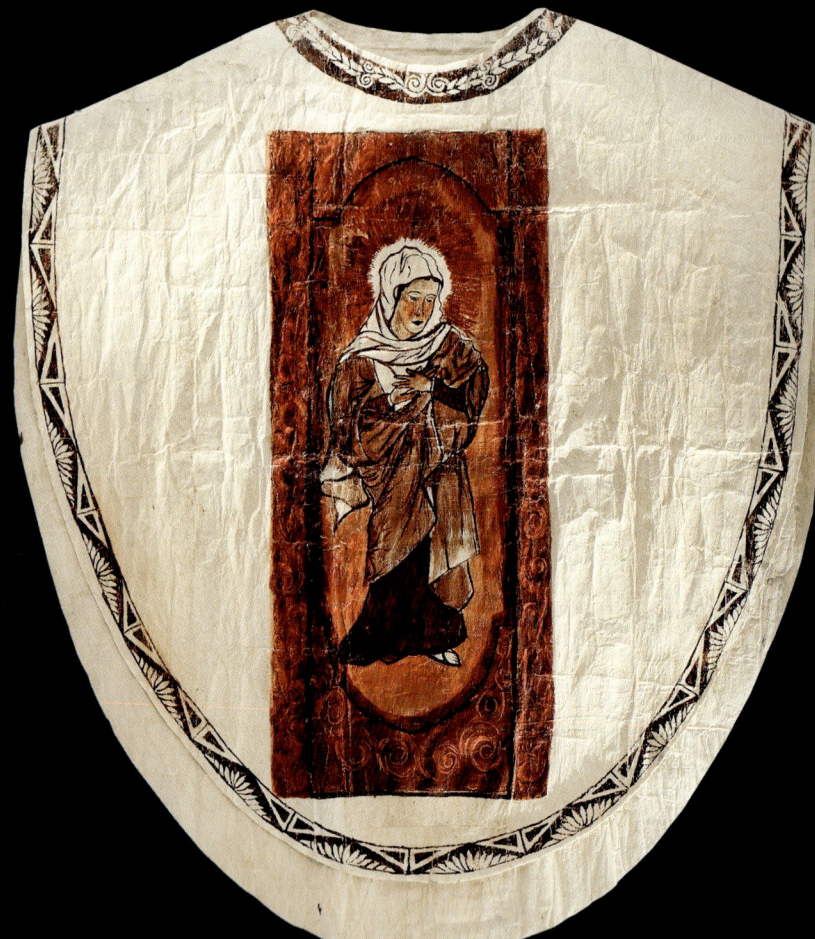

Tapa chasuble

Since it was introduced in the early nineteenth century, Christianity has permeated the social and cultural life of Pacific peoples: their indigenous arts have been influenced by its literature, teachings, and iconography. Conversely, the rituals and trappings of Christianity in the Pacific have been coloured by the art forms and cultural practices of these island nations.

This chasuble, a priest's vestment worn for communion services, is made from tapa (decorated bark cloth), painted freehand with both Christian and Tongan imagery. The Tongan pattern, known as Tokelau feletoa, and a motif possibly representing olive branches decorate the border. On the front of the garment is an image of the Virgin Mary; on the back is an image of Christ.

The chasuble was made in Tonga for Father John Faisandier in 1978, to mark his ordination as a Catholic priest in the Hutt Valley. It was then taken to St Mary's seminary, in Hawke's Bay.

Tapa (decorated bark cloth) chasuble
1978
Made in Ma'ufanga Village, painted in Vaololoa Village by Mata'itini Tu'akoi, Fatima Cheeseman, and 'Etita Tausinga Tonga
Bark cloth, dyes
1060 x 920 mm
Gift of the Society of Mary, Wellington, 2002

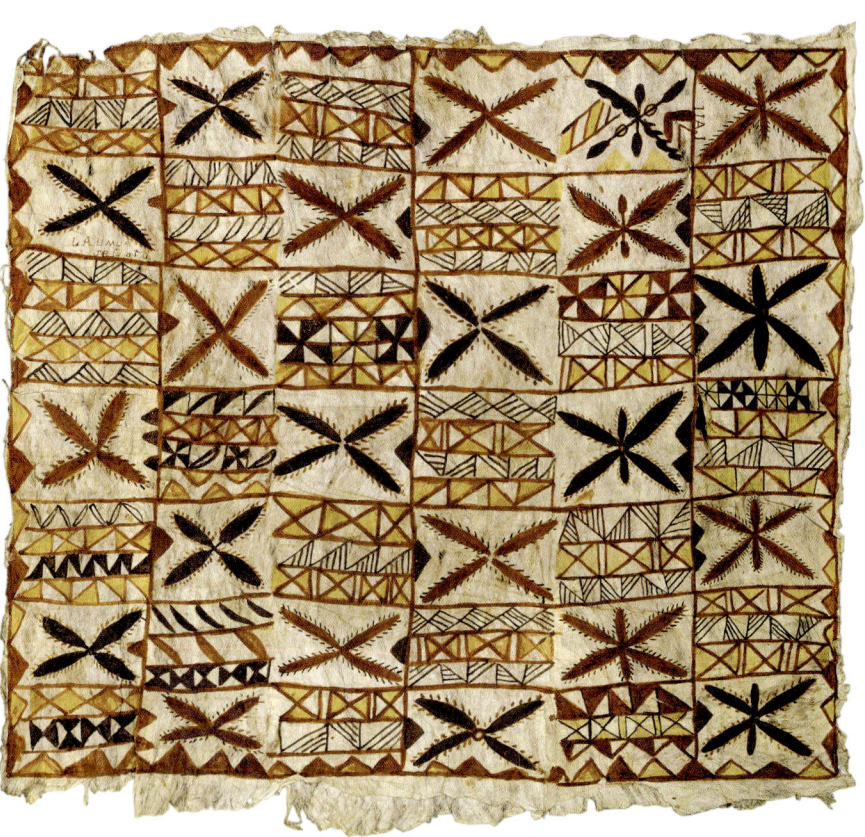

Siapo mamanu
(freehand decorated bark cloth)

Siapo is the Samoan name for decorated cloth made from the u'a (paper mulberry tree). First, the bark is peeled off the tree in strips. The inner bark is separated, scraped clean, and pounded, then pasted together to make the size of cloth required. The piece is decorated in freehand or by taking rubbings off a relief pattern carved into a board.

Siapo mamanu is bark cloth that has been decorated freehand, featuring plant and animal motifs. The creative flair of siapo-makers is demonstrated in their arrangement of the motifs, and their clever use of a restricted colour palette. The dyes are made from various plants and trees, and an earth ochre called 'ele.

This siapo mamanu dates from the 1890s, when siapo-making was at its height. It is part of a major collection of Māori and Pacific artefacts gifted to the museum in 1913 by Alexander Turnbull.

Siapo mamanu
(freehand decorated bark cloth)
late 19th century
Samoa
Bark cloth
1370 x 1275 mm
Gift of Alexander Turnbull, 1913

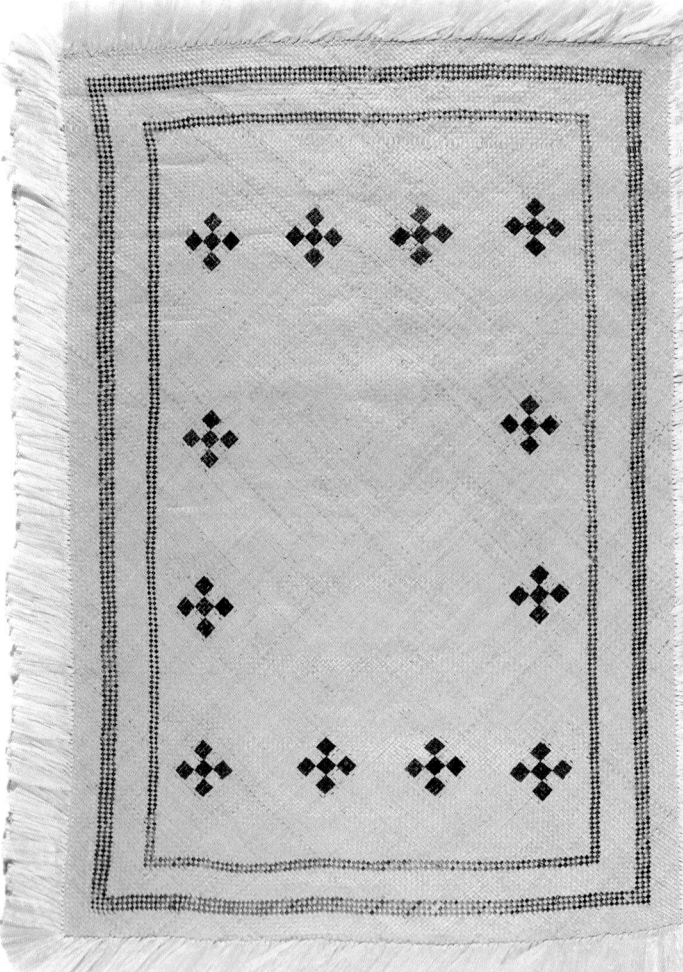

Kie tau (fine mat)

The making of kie tau requires particular preparation to ensure that the pandanus is smooth and flexible. These hand-woven mats have a special place in Tokelauan society, as they are worn and presented at weddings and used in burials.

This kie tau, made in New Zealand, reflects a community's innovations with materials available. The main body of the mat and its border pattern and decorative motifs are made from pandanus imported from Tokelau. The thick outer fringe is very similar to the kanava bark fibre found in Tokelau, but in fact was obtained from packing-case material at a car-assembly plant in New Zealand.

Although some of the materials have changed, the way they have been processed and woven together, and how they are used, contribute greatly to the mat's value. Mats such as this, using contemporary materials, continue to have a significant cultural role in Tokelauan communities, whether in New Zealand or in Tokelau.

Kie tau (fine mat)
c. 1991

Made by Telesia Lino, Katalina Paselio, Maselina Pereira, Fetu Perez, Malia Sesale, Vito Koloi, Susana Koloi, Matalena Atonio, Valelia Lafaele, and Kolopa Isle of Ko Fatu Paepae o Lower Hutt
Tokelau/New Zealand

Pandanus, synthetic fibre

1510 x 2000 mm

Purchased 1993

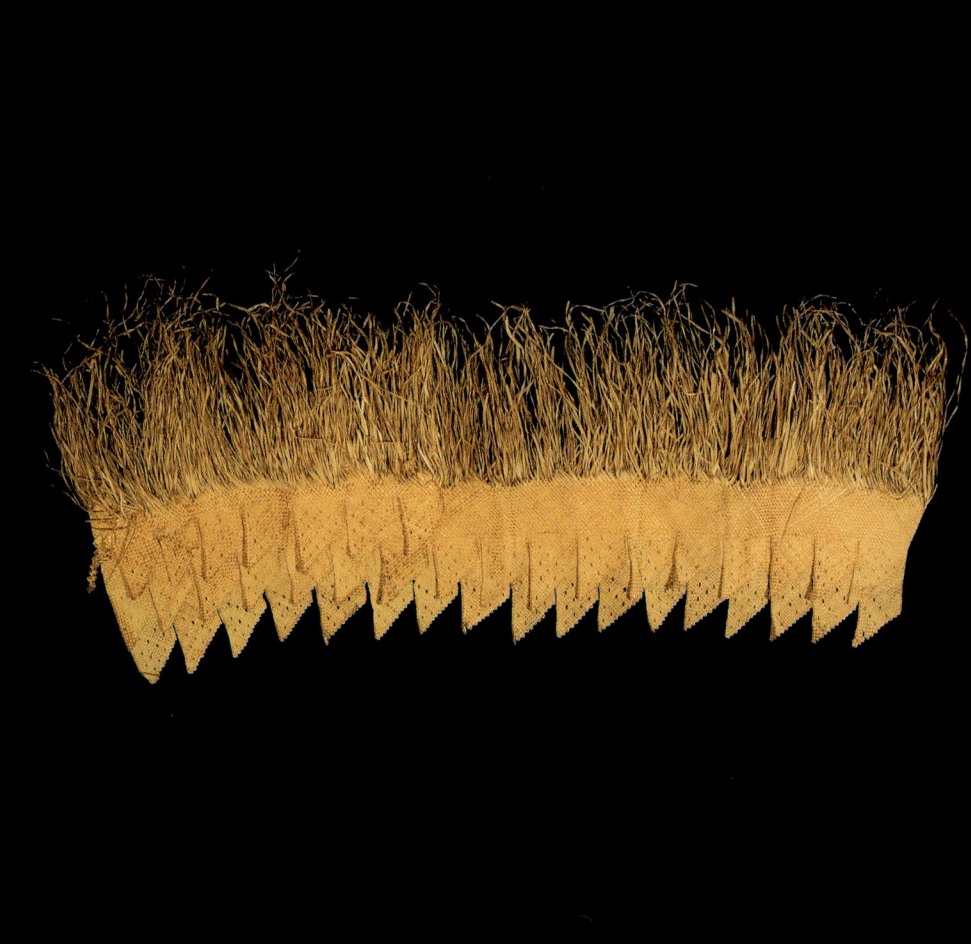

Unfinished overskirt

Waist ornaments and overskirts of various kinds are a mark of Tongan identity in New Zealand today. But this unfinished waist ornament was made more than two hundred years ago. It was probably collected during Captain Cook's first visit to Tonga in 1773.

The garment was being worked from the bottom up; the tabs would have pointed downwards, and the loose fibres would have been used to form the waistband. The plaiting is complex; Tongan weavers today do not know how to make such an intricate garment. Cook may have had this particular piece in mind when he wrote: 'they have also a kind of worked apron which is curious on account of the time it must take to make one.'

At one time the overskirt belonged to Queen Victoria and then to Edward VII, who gave it to the Imperial Institute. It is possible that Cook himself presented it to King George III.

Unfinished overskirt
late 18th century
Tonga
Hibiscus fibre
590 x 1140mm
Gift of the Imperial Institute, 1955

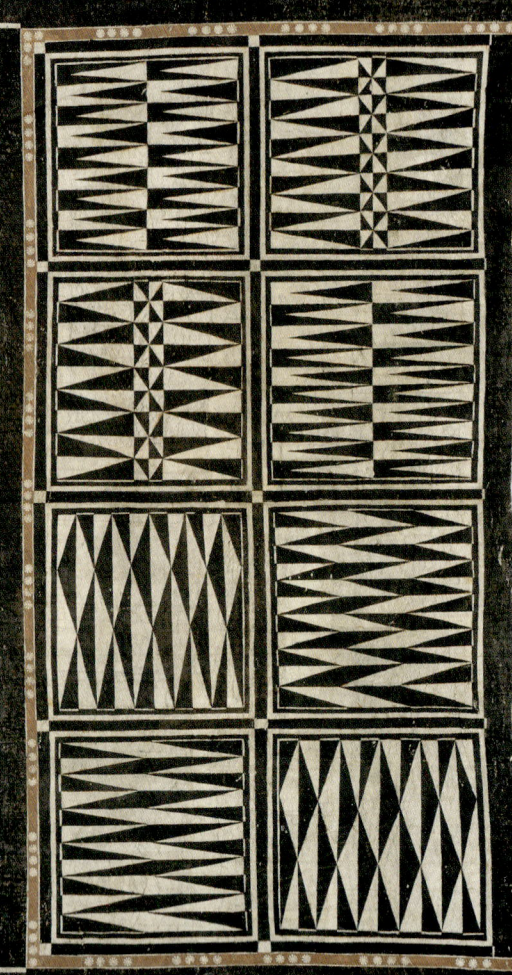

Masi room divider

Masi is the Fijian name for decorated bark cloth and is made exclusively by women there. Its uses are very diverse, including room dividers (as here), garments, turbans, wall art, bedding, and ceremonial gifts. The different colours used reflect a person's rank in society, with white or brown masi restricted to the families of chiefs.

The method of decoration differs from place to place, and has changed over the years. In earlier times, stencils were made from green pandanus leaves. Today, they tend to be ready-made and reusable, often cut from X-ray film because of its durability. In the eastern parts of Fiji, women use rubbing tablets rather than stencils, reflecting a Tongan influence.

Although masi designs tend to be unique to specific locations, women take their own distinctive designs to their new homes when they marry. Thus, finished masi pieces often combine designs from various places.

Masi (decorated bark cloth) room divider
c. 1900
Fiji
Bark cloth
2100 x 4180 mm
Acquisition history unknown

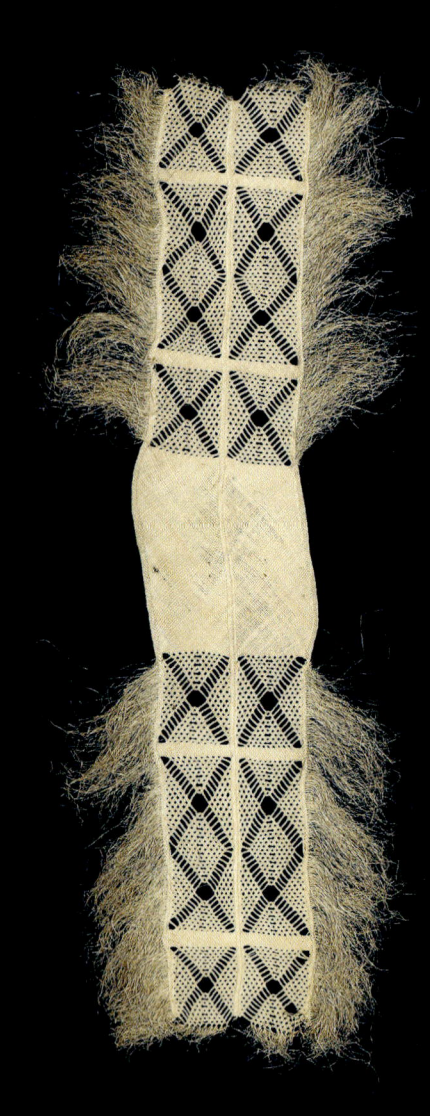

Costume mat, Vanuatu

The women of the northern Vanuatu islands of Ambae, Maewo, and Pentecost have long been famous for their mat-making skills. Their products include small, fine items of clothing, floor coverings, and large mats used in ceremonial presentations.

Many of the mats from these islands are dyed a distinctive red or purple colour. Most of the fine costume mats were worn by men as loincloths. A few, like this one, are undyed and instead feature openwork patterns. They were worn by women as head-coverings.

Mats have maintained their importance in Vanuatu society, where they are used as items of exchange on great occasions, such as weddings. The mats are significant symbolic and ritual objects, and have been described as the 'soul of the people'. The writer Grace Molisa has called Vanuatu a 'mat society' and has pointed to parallels with other Pacific island societies, where fine mats are also central to ritual and ceremony.

Costume mat
late 19th century
Vanuatu
Plant fibres
220 x 1160 mm
Gift of Mrs Swabey, 1961

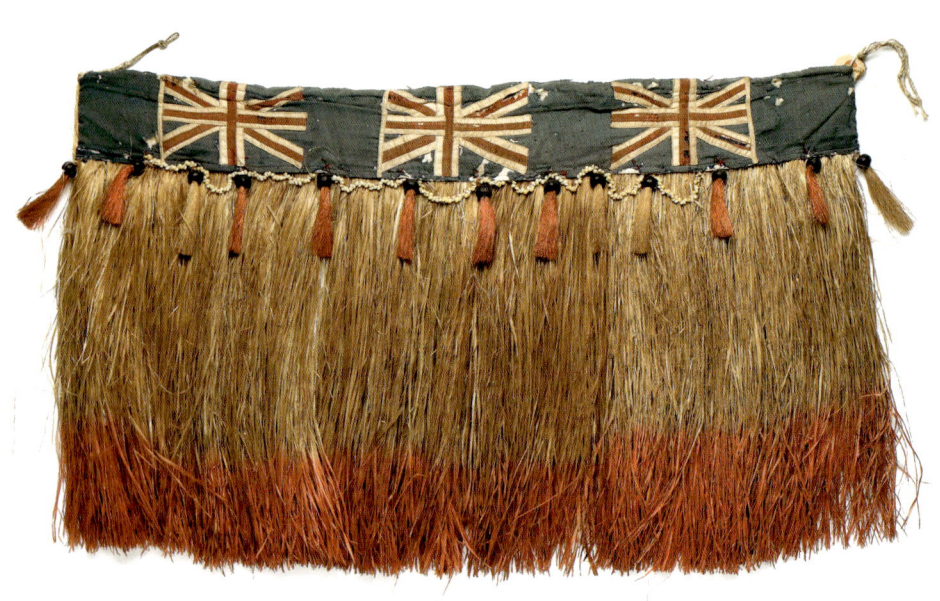

Titi (dance skirt)

A skirt worn by dancers, the titi is usually made from leaves and other plant material. This titi, however, makes skilful use of both appliqué and weaving. Pieces of coloured cloth have been sewn to form images of the Union Jack on the waistband, and the skirt is made of hibiscus-bark fibre.

William Churchward, the British consul to Samoa, commented in the 1880s on the British flag's impact on Samoan fashion, noting it had 'suddenly made its appearance in the form of big handkerchiefs, which were used either as lava-lavas or shawls'. He also recorded that an outraged British patriot tried to confiscate every Union Jack he saw worn by a Samoan, either 'paying him for it or giving him something of less pronounced individuality in exchange'.

This titi, made to mark the visit of the Prince of Wales to Samoa in 1920, pays an ingenious and respectful tribute to the royal visitor.

Titi (dance skirt)
1920
Samoa
Hibiscus fibres, cloth, shells, seeds
520 x 845 mm
Gift of E. Furness, 1961

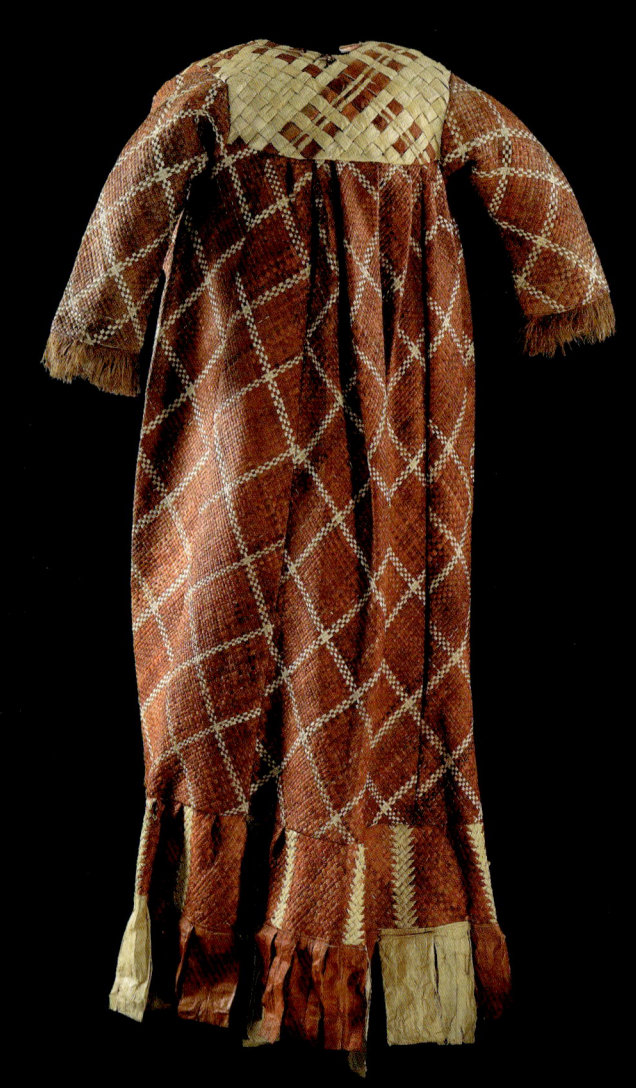

'Mother Hubbard' dress

A mix of indigenous Pacific materials and introduced European style comes together in this 'Mother Hubbard' style of dress.

From the early nineteenth century, encounters between people of the Pacific and Europeans led to a vigorous exchange of ideas, technologies, and products. Missionaries introduced new concepts of modesty and different kinds of clothing. Long dresses, shirts, and jackets were frequently unsuitable for the hot climate, but they were often worn, and sometimes eagerly sought. In some parts of the Pacific, European dress became a status symbol, or a marker of identity with a group such as a church.

This dress, made about 1900, is attributed to Tuvalu on the basis of the distinctive yellow- and red-dyed pandanus, typical of the weaving from this area. The garment has been made from sections of pandanus matting, cut to shape, and then machine-stitched. Pearl-shell buttons add a finishing touch. Fraying around the neck and armholes indicates it has been worn quite often.

Dress
c. 1900
Tuvalu (attributed)
Pandanus-leaf strips, European cloth, thread
1450 x 760 mm
Purchased from A. Hannah, 1915

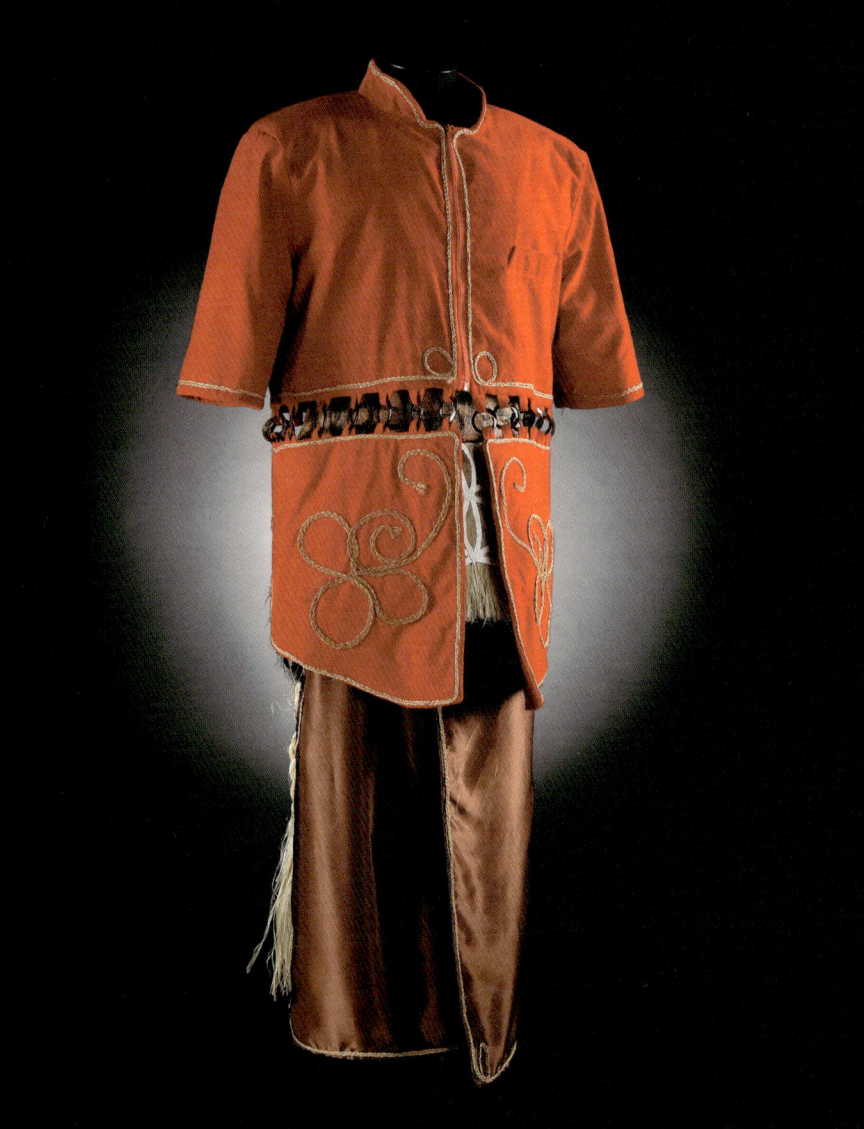

Man's suit

This award-winning suit is derived from the formal modern garments of Samoan, Tongan, and Fijian men. With its vibrant colours and creative use of both natural and manufactured materials, it also reflects recent trends in contemporary women's costumes.

The three-piece suit comprises a satin-lined red velvet jacket, a brown satin lavalava (wrap-around skirt), and a ta'ovala (a decorative overskirt). The ta'ovala features brown-patterned Tongan tapa (bark cloth) and a thick fringe of fau (hibiscus-bark fibre), overlaid by a lattice of linked plastic petals or leaves. The lavalava and jacket are decorated with spirals of sennit (coconut fibre), and coconut-shell rings are used in an openwork waistband around the jacket. The lavalava's edges are finished with a long, plaited strand of coconut-fibre cord; at its ends are two long plaits of fau.

The work of Asomaliu Fou Tagiilima, the suit's designer, is characterised by this innovative combination of materials and cultural styles.

Man's suit
1990s
Made by Asomaliu Fou Tagiilima
Samoa/New Zealand
Satin, velvet, bark cloth, hibiscus-bark fibre, plastic, coconut fibre
Skirt: 440 x 860 mm
jacket: 1040 x 1000 mm
Purchased 1998 with New Zealand Lottery Grants Board funds

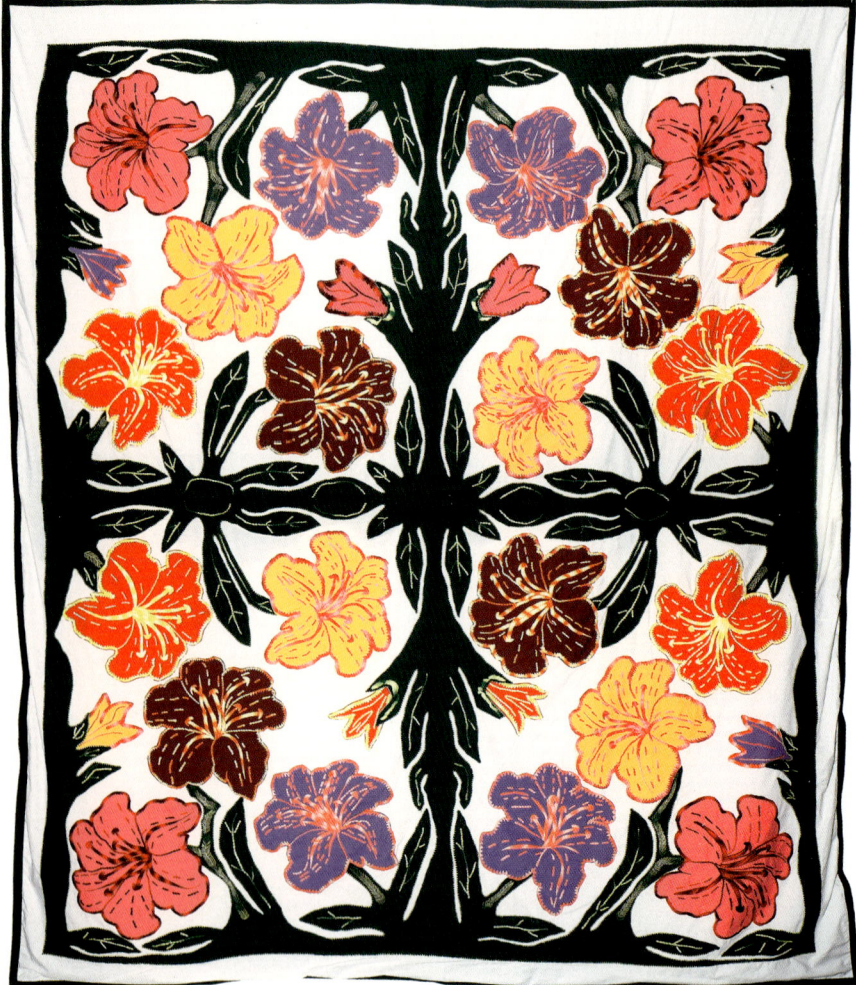

Tīvaevae (quilt)

Tīvaevae are made by women throughout eastern Polynesia. Quilt-making was probably introduced by missionary wives some time in the nineteenth century, and tīvaevae became so popular that they eventually replaced woven textiles and bark cloth as the most important form of women's wealth.

Tīvaevae are used domestically to decorate beds and furniture, but have a more significant role as gifts at haircutting ceremonies and weddings. Making them involves two main sewing techniques: patchwork and appliqué.

This example, known as a tīvaevae tātaura, uses a particularly elaborate form of appliqué incorporating several different stitches. It was designed and cut by Vaine Ngaro, president of the Cannons Creek Vainetine (women's group) in Porirua, and sewn by the group. According to Ngaro, 'each blossom symbolises our cultural and spiritual values. The women who work together in harmony have shared in this creation of the "New Beginning".'

Blossoms of the New Beginning
2001

Tīvaevae tātaura (quilt) made by Vaine Ngaro, Jasmine Underhill, Greta Daniels, Noo Hosking, Toka Heeney, Ina Makirere, Rua McGloughlin, Tehea Katu, Na Isaia, Teremoana Emile, and Urau Pouaru of Cannons Creek Vainetine
Cook Islands/New Zealand

Cloth

2530 x 2190 mm

Purchased 2001 with New Zealand Lottery Grants Board funds

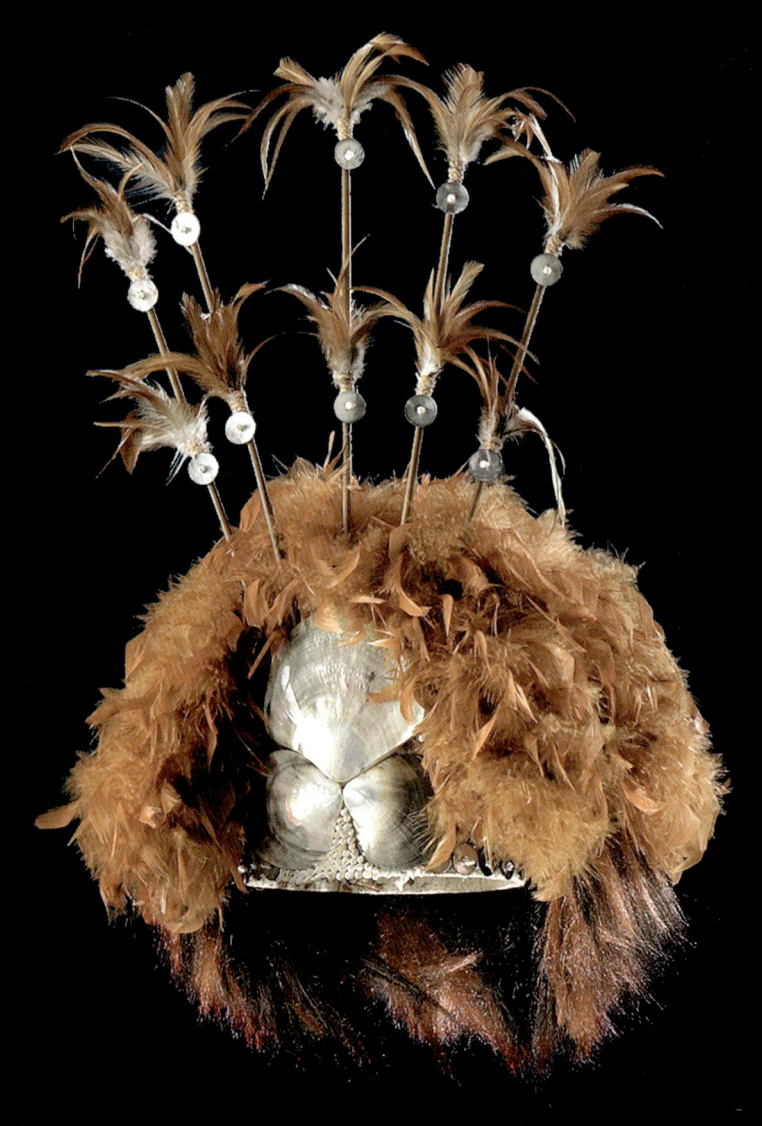

Tuiga (headdress)

The magnificent dance costumes of Samoan taupou (daughters of chiefs) inspired Paula Chan Cheuk to create the work shown here, a costume comprising this headdress and a fine mat dress (page 92).

Adorned with feathers, the tuiga is made so that it sits precariously on the dancer's head. Its elaborate construction ensures that the wearer maintains an upright posture and moves gracefully. In the nineteenth and early twentieth centuries, tuiga were made of separate elements that were put together only when the headdress was to be worn. Today, it is more like an elaborate ready-made hat, with all the pieces permanently assembled.

Paula Chan Cheuk is widely known in the Pacific community for her elegant synthesis of Pacific, Asian, and European styles. This costume was created for the Traditional Wear section of the 1997 Miss Samoa New Zealand competition for Susan Pa'u, who went on to win the title.

Tuiga (headdress)
1997
Made by Paula Chan Cheuk
Samoa/New Zealand
Pandanus, shell, feathers
560 x 470 mm
Purchased 1997 with New Zealand
Lottery Grants Board funds

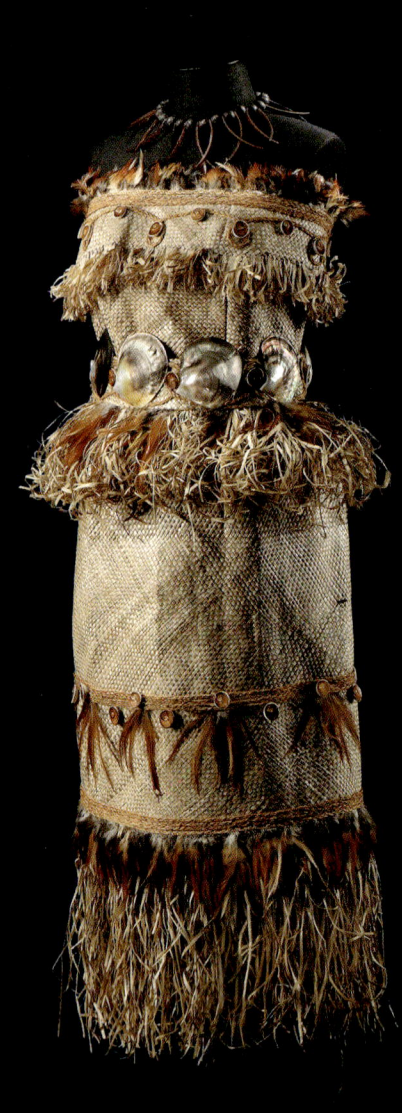

'ie tōga dress

This dress made from an 'ie tōga (fine mat), along with the headdress shown on page 90, comprise a costume created for the Traditional Wear section of the Miss Samoa New Zealand competition (1997). Its creator, Paula Chan Cheuk, was inspired by the dance costumes of Samoan taupou (daughters of chiefs).

The 'ie tōga was woven from strips of pandanus fibre and decorated with shells, fibre, and 'afa (coconut-fibre cord). 'ie tōga are highly valued in Samoa, and are presented as precious gifts at weddings, funerals, and other important occasions.

The waist garment is decorated with eight pearl shells, feathers, pandanus fibre, and cat's-eye shells. The 'ie tōga and 'afa are from Si'usega village on Upolu, and the feathers are from New Zealand. The small cat's-eye shells were collected by Chan Cheuk from a beach near her Auckland home.

'ie tōga (fine mat) dress
1997
Made by Paula Chan Cheu
Samoa/New Zealand
Pandanus, shell, feathers
1165 x 485 mm
Purchased 1997 with New Zealand
Lottery Grants Board funds

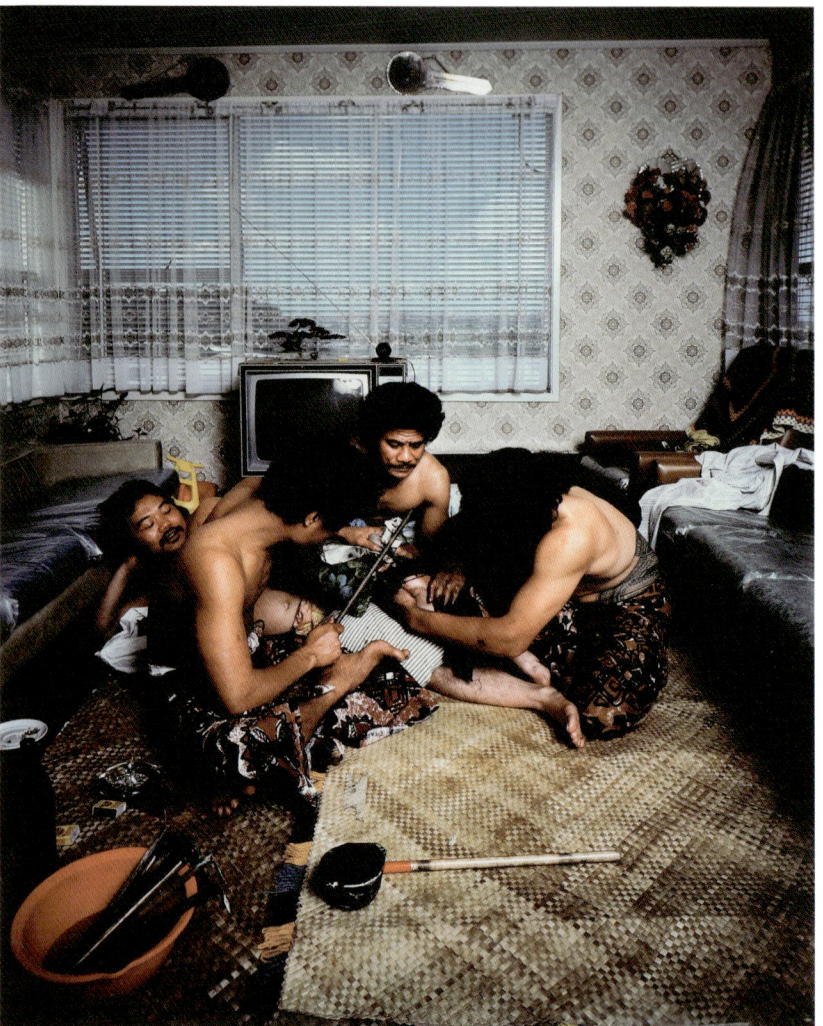

Samoan tattooing

The tatau (tattoo) worn by Samoan males is called the pe'a; the female equivalent is the malu. These forms of tatau are an integral part of the ritual and ceremonial aspects of Samoan society. The pe'a is a set of markings from the waist to the knee. It is made up of fine parallel line-work and areas of shade, and incorporates a range of motifs and intricate geometric patterns.

The word pe'a also refers to the fruit-eating bat known as the flying fox. Samoan writer Albert Wendt suggests that the male tatau is so named because it has the same charcoal colour as the flying fox, and symbolises the bat's courageous, cheeky nature.

Since the 1970s, photographer Mark Adams has documented the work of Samoan tattooists in New Zealand, such as Su'a Sulu'ape Paulo. In this photograph, Adams captures a new urban context for Samoan tatau, which has spread across the Pacific and beyond.

Mark Adams
(born 1949), New Zealand
7.10.78. Triangle Road, Massey, West Auckland. Tattooing Tom. Tufuga tātatau: Su'a Sulu'ape Paulo; Solo: Arona and Leo Maselino
1978
Colour photograph, C-type print
306 x 242 mm
Purchased 1993

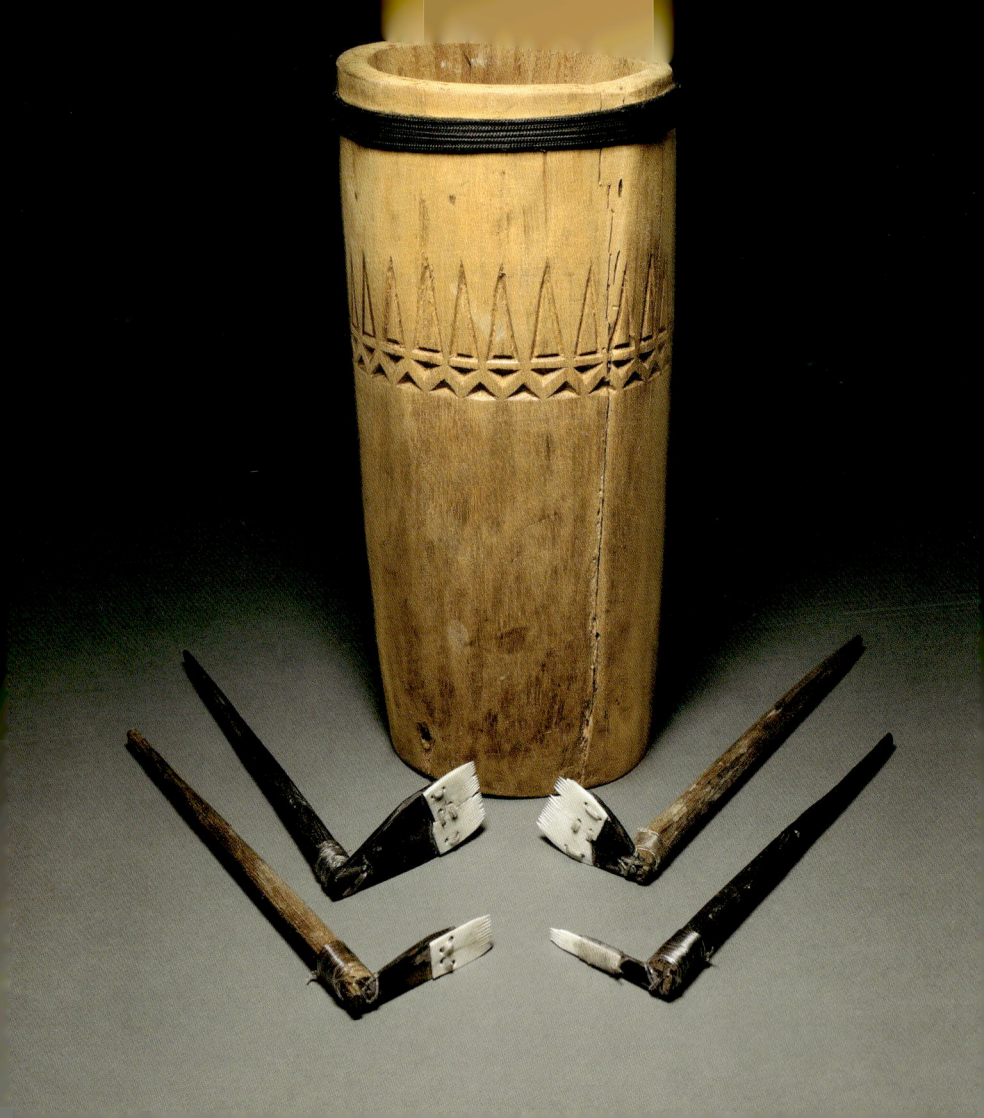

'au tā (tattooing tools)

The tool kit of the tufuga tātatau
(Samoan tattooing expert) contains small,
carefully crafted tools. They are precision
instruments, designed to create the
beautiful lines and motifs of tatau. The
'au are small bone combs with sharpened
teeth fixed to a shell plate, then attached
to a wooden handle. They come in various
widths, each able to render different
kinds of line. Some combs fill in large
dark areas; others make very fine lines
and dots.

When not in use, the tools are stored
in a tunuma, made from a hollowed-out
pandanus trunk. This set of tattooing
tools was made by Su'a Sulu'ape Petelo,
a leading tufuga tātatau.

For several decades, Samoan tattooists
have practised their art on people across
the Pacific, and in the United States
and Europe. The distinctive markings of
Samoan tatau, and the intriguing tools of
the artist's trade, see tufuga tātatau highly
sought after at tattooing conventions and
festivals throughout the world.

'au tā (tattooing tools)
1996
Made by Su'a Sulu'ape Petelo, Samoa
Wood, shell, nylon, bone
Tools: various sizes
container: 294 mm height,
135 mm diameter
Purchased 1996 with New Zealand
Lottery Grants Board funds

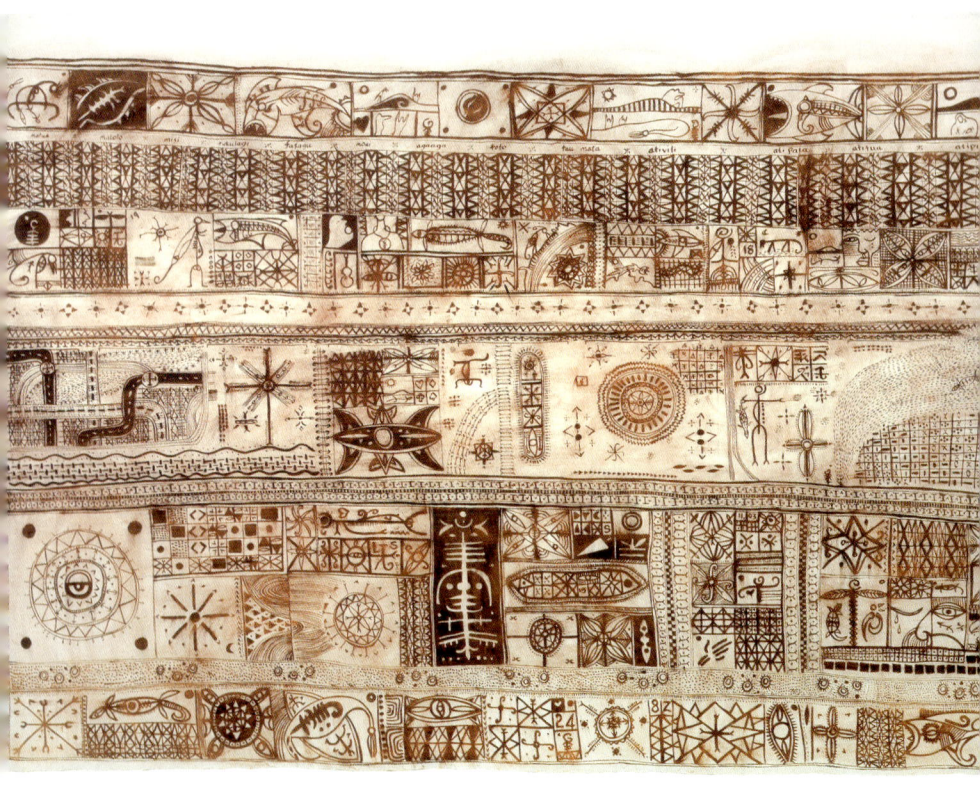

John Pule

Many artists of Pacific descent in New Zealand explore the histories of their peoples, the circumstances of migration, and what it means to be Pacific Islanders and New Zealanders.

The work of Niuean-born New Zealander John Pule is grounded in hiapo – an early type of decorated bark cloth from Niue (page 68). The hand-painted patterns of hiapo comprise sprawling trails of leafy vines, as well as motifs and images whose associated stories are now forgotten.

Pule's paintings also draw on a contemporary iconography. Here, the storyboard-like construction contains many kinds of image: landscapes and bodies, structures within structures, cartographic elements, concentric circles, watchful eyes, and grotesque motifs. All connect to the death of the artist's young daughter Zaiya. The title, *Episode AA – 940035 Tukulagi Haaku*, includes the reference number of a CAT-scan report made for Zaiya at the time of her illness.

John Pule
(born 1962), Niue/New Zealand
Episode AA – 940035 Tukulagi Haaku
1994
Oil paint on canvas
3040 x 4230 mm
Purchased 1997 with New Zealand Lottery Grants Board funds

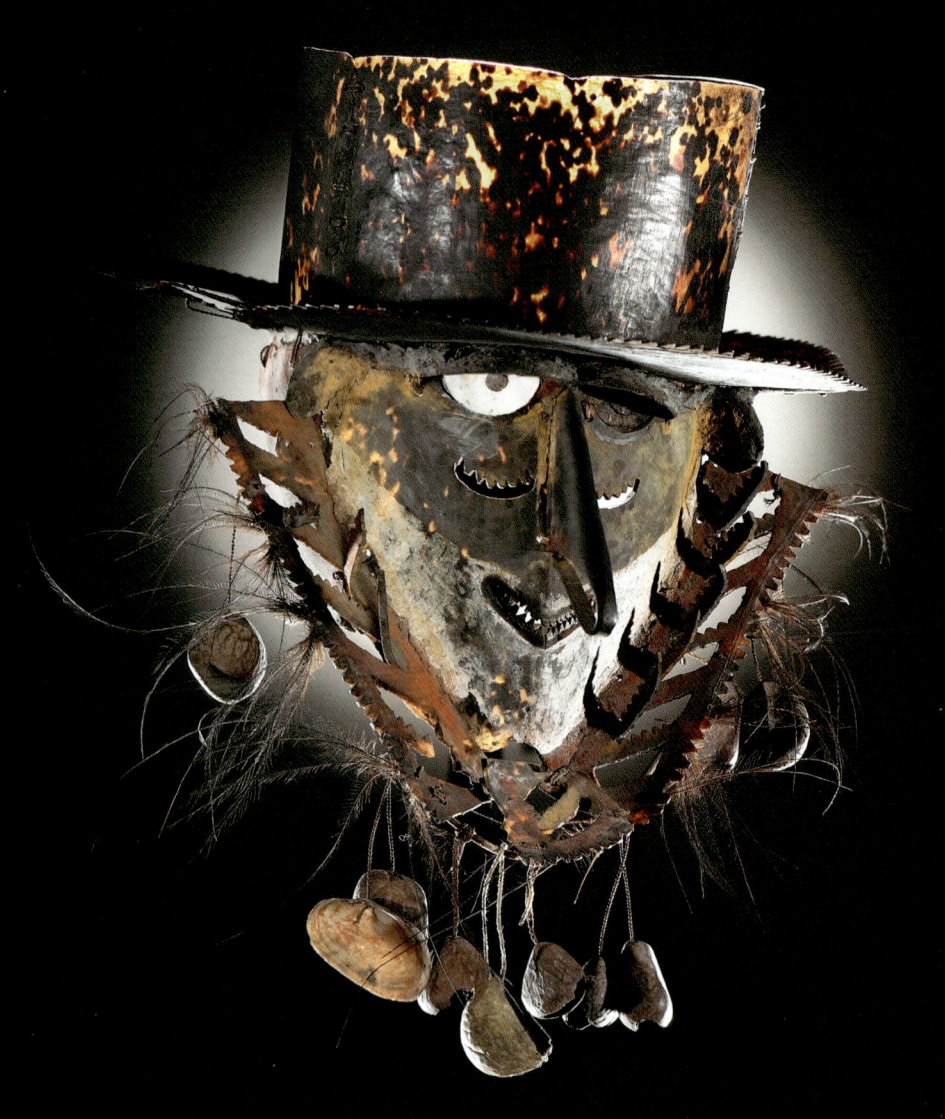

Torres Strait Islands mask

Masks, especially those made from turtle shell, were a feature of Torres Strait Islands culture. This remarkable mask is unusual among Torres Strait masks in the way it incorporates a broad-brimmed European-style hat.

Nothing is known about how this mask was used, or whether in fact it was made especially for presentation to a visiting British dignitary. The early 1870s were a time of rapid change in the Torres Strait Islands, as the islanders began to accept Christianity, and contact with Europeans greatly increased. Te Papa's Pacific collection also includes several striking early adaptations of European hat styles in other forms — actual hats, or carvings of people wearing hats.

The mask was part of a collection of Australian and New Guinean artefacts given to the Colonial Museum by George Phipps, Marquess of Normanby, a former governor of Queensland and Governor of New Zealand from 1874 to 1878.

Mask
c. 1870
Murray Island, Torres Strait Islands, Australia
Wood, turtle shell, plant fibre, nuts, shells, feathers, pigment
374 x 355 x 430 mm
Gift of the Marquess of Normanby, 1875

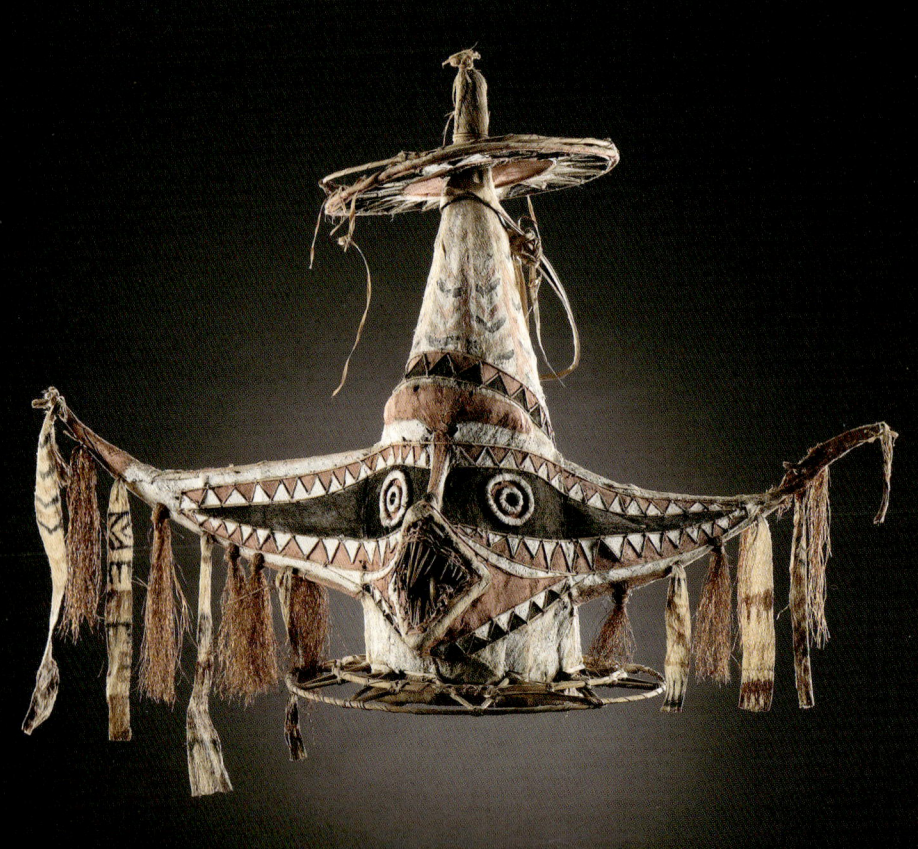

Eharo (dance mask)

The eharo was a dance mask worn during the Heheve. This was a grand cycle of ceremonies that dominated the ritual and artistic lives of the Western Elema people of the Gulf of Papua during the early twentieth century.

In many areas, masks were worn during the rituals of men's secret societies. Women, children, and uninitiated men believed the masked figures were dangerous supernatural beings. However, eharo represent the light-hearted and sometimes comic side of the Heheve cycle. Anyone could make such a mask and wear it. There was no secrecy or sense of disguise about eharo; women knew they were made and worn by men, and who those men were.

Eharo represented all manner of totemic creatures – birds, fish, insects, reptiles, dogs, trees, even mushrooms and jellyfish. A mask was usually topped by a representation of its creature. The circle on top of this mask, now lacking its decoration, may represent a jellyfish.

Eharo (dance mask)
early 20th century
Orokolo, Gulf Province,
Papua New Guinea
Cane, bark cloth, plant fibre, pigment
570 x 890 x 330 mm
Purchased 1914

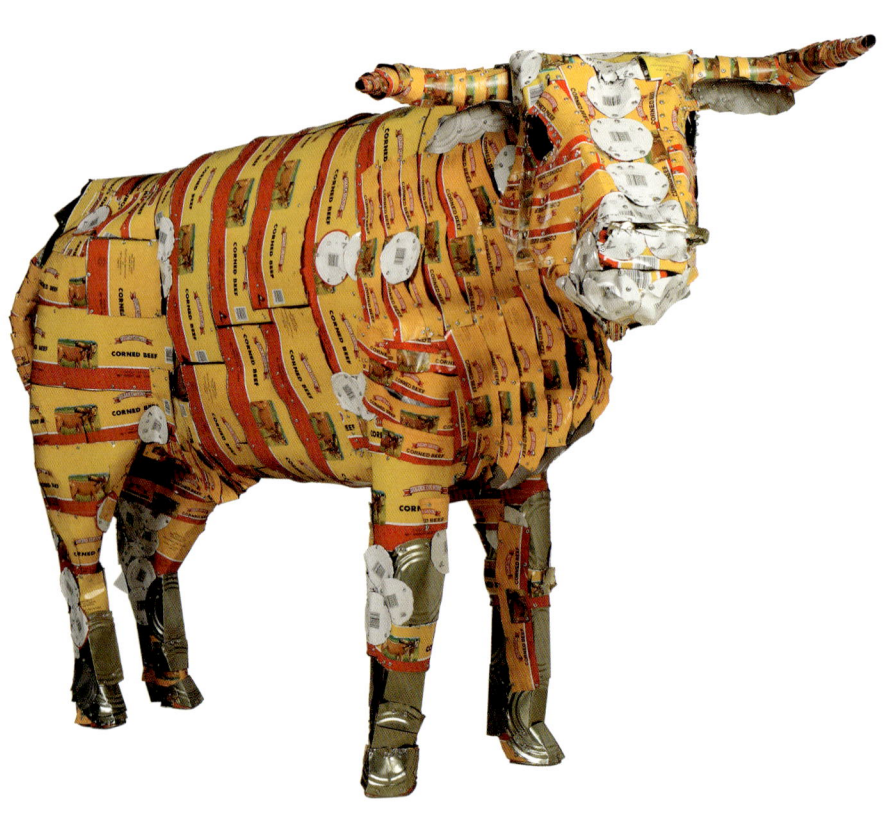

Michel Tuffery

For decades, pisupo or imported tinned food has taken the place of local foods as a prestigious item eaten and gifted at Samoan feasts, weddings, funerals, and other special occasions. Michel Tuffery's artwork is a commentary on this trend.

Like many artists of Pacific descent living in New Zealand, Tuffery draws his themes from the wider Pacific and its history, often focusing on issues relating to its people and their changing environment. Through *Pisupo lua afe* (*Corned beef 2000*), he raises questions about how colonial economies have affected Pacific peoples, and whether foreign intervention encourages independence or in fact fosters dependency.

This work was the first of a series of cattle sculptures that Tuffery has made. It was acquired by Te Papa as part of an initiative to document a new generation of artists of Pacific descent in New Zealand. Since then, *Pisupo lua afe* has been a popular work in Te Papa's *Mana Pasifika* exhibition.

Michel Tuffery
(born 1966), New Zealand
Pisupo lua afe (Corned beef 2000)
1994
Tin cans, rivets
1150 x 650 x 2170 mm
Purchased 1995

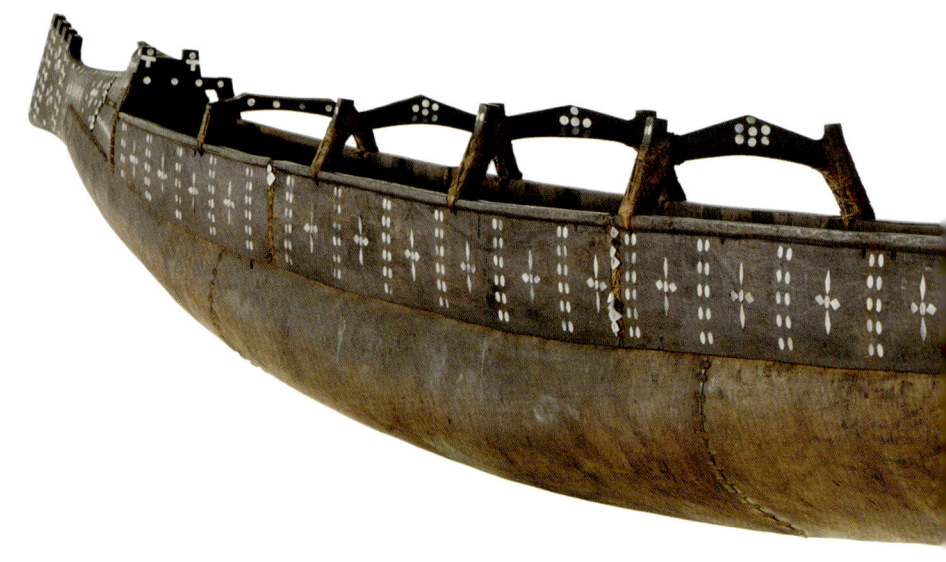

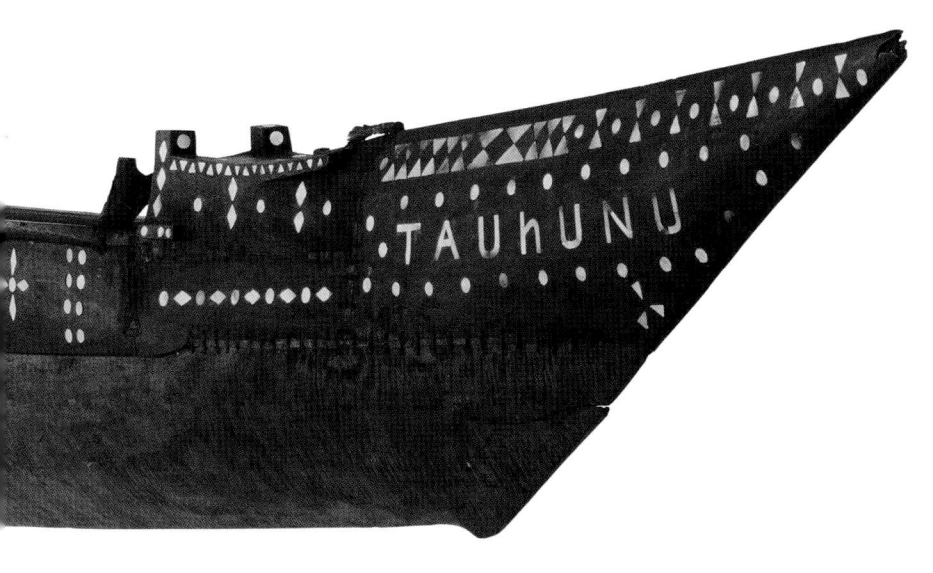

Tauhunu

Tauhunu is an outrigger vaka (canoe), originally sent from the Cook Islands for display at the Christchurch International Exhibition in 1906. Its name, inlaid with pearl shell, is that of the main village of Manihiki, the Cook Islands atoll where it was made.

The vaka was used for fishing and other short voyages, mainly inside the atoll's lagoon. It could be either paddled or sailed, powered by one or two inverted triangular sails. The hull comprises several wooden sections sewn together with coconut fibre. The outrigger float (not shown here) would have been attached to the main hull by two or more booms. The hull could also be tied to another hull to create a more stable double-hulled canoe, similar to a catamaran.

Vaka are still used in the Cook Islands, but the quality of the workmanship evident in *Tauhunu*, with its precise tapering and immaculate finish, is not matched in modern ones.

Tauhunu, vaka (canoe)
late 19th century
Manihiki, northern Cook Islands
Wood, coconut fibre, pearl shell
430 x 8860 mm
Purchased 1907